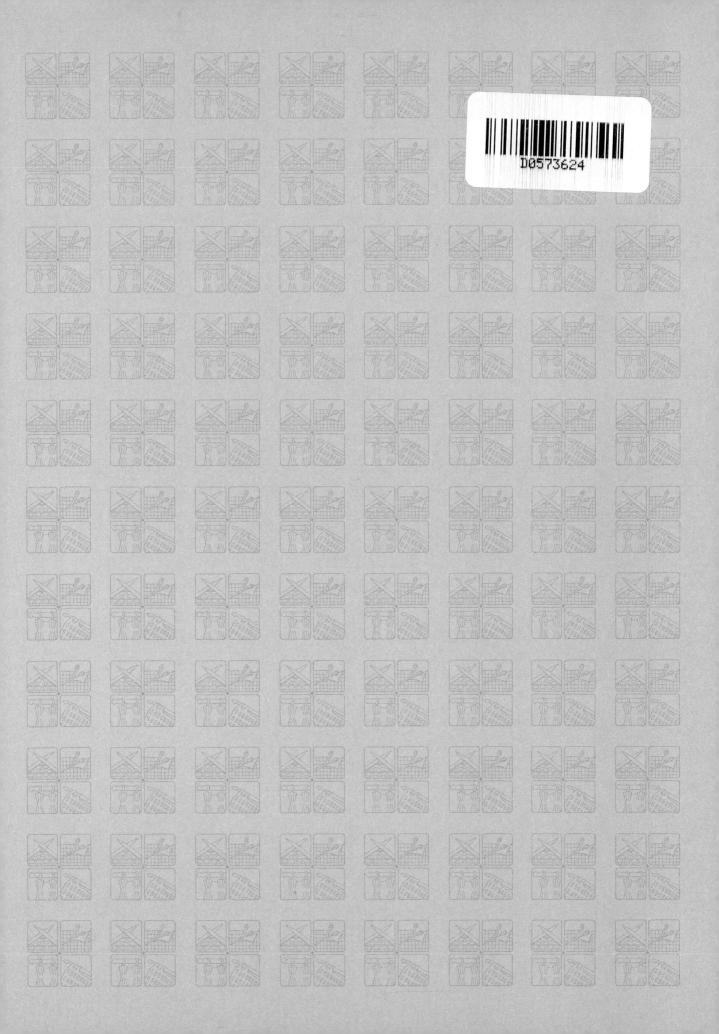

Stitch by Stitch

Volume 7

TORSTAR BOOKS

NEW YORK · TORONTO

Stitch by Stitch

TORSTAR BOOKS INC.
41 MADISON AVENUE
SUITE 2900
NEW YORK, NY 10010

Knitting and crochet abbreviations

approx = approximately
beg = begin(ning)
ch = chain(s)
cm = centimeter(s)
cont = continue(ing)
dc = double crochet
dec = decrease(e)(ing)
dtr = double triple
foll = follow(ing)
g = gram(s)
grp = group(s)
hdc = half double
   crochet

in = inch(es)
inc = increas(e)(ing)
K = knit
oz = ounce(s)
P = purl
patt = pattern
psso = pass slipped
   stitch over
rem = remain(ing)
rep = repeat
RS = right side
sc = single crochet
sl = slip

sl st = slip stitch
sp = space(s)
st(s) = stitch(es)
tbl = through back of
   loop(s)
tog = together
tr = triple crochet
WS = wrong side
wyib = with yarn in
   back
wyif = with yarn in front
yd = yard(s)
yo = yarn over

A guide to the pattern sizes

		10	12	14	16	18	20
Bust	in	32½	34	36	38	40	42
	cm	83	87	92	97	102	107
Waist	in	25	26½	28	30	32	34
	cm	64	67	71	76	81	87
Hips	in	34½	36	38	40	42	44
	cm	88	92	97	102	107	112

Torstar Books also offers a range of acrylic book stands, designed to keep instructional books such as *Stitch by Stitch* open, flat and upright while leaving the hands free for practical work.

For information write to Torstar Books Inc., 41 Madison Avenue, Suite 2900, New York, NY 10010.

Library of Congress Cataloging in Publication Data
Main entry under title:

Stitch by stitch.

   Includes index.
   1. Needlework. I. Torstar Books (Firm)
TT705.S74 1984   746.4   84-111
ISBN 0-920269-00-1 (set)

9876543

© Marshall Cavendish Limited 1985

Printed in Belgium

ISBN 0−920269−07−9   (Volume 7)

Contents

Crochet / COURSE 29

More lace edgings

In this course we show you some more lace edgings which can either be worked directly onto the edge of your fabric or be worked separately and sewn onto the edge of a completed garment or household item. For example, you could make a separate edging in crochet cotton or a fine knitting yarn to go around the edge of a plain collar or across the yoke of a girl's dress. Similarly, you could use any of these edgings to trim the cuffs of a fabric shirt, the hem of a skirt, or the edge of a crib blanket or shawl.

To work the edgings separately you begin, as usual, by making a length of chain. To calculate the number of chains required, measure all around the border of your fabric and make the length of chain equivalent to this measurement. When checking the length of the chain, avoid stretching it. Remember to add the appropriate number of turning chains. This number will, of course, vary depending on the stitch worked in the first row of your edging. For example you will need to make 1 extra chain for single crochet, 3 for double crochet, and so on. When you are working an edging directly onto the fabric, you usually begin by working a row of single crochet. The number of single crochets required will depend on the type of yarn and stitch used for the main fabric. Sometimes a pattern will specify the number of stitches to be worked around the edge of the garment; but as a general guide you will find that working one stitch into each stitch and each row end on a single crochet fabric will make a neat, even, base row on which to work the edging, whereas you may have to work 2 stitches into each row end on a more open fabric.

Ray Duns

Lace-shell edging

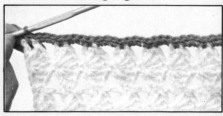

1 Begin this pretty shell border by working a row of single crochet along the edge of the fabric. Use a multiple of 4 stitches, plus 3 extra.

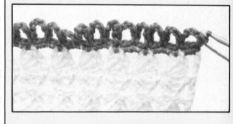

2 Work the first row of the edging by making 5-chain loops, linked by working a single crochet into every other stitch all along the edge, making sure that you work the last single crochet into the top of the turning chain, or last stitch at the end of the row. In this way you make a series of 5-chain loops.

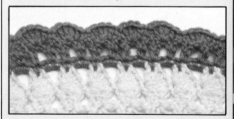

3 Begin the next row by working 5 doubles into the third chain in the first loop to make the first shell. (No turning chain is needed.) Now continue to work a single crochet into the 3rd chain of the next loop, followed by a shell into the 3rd chain of the following loop, alternately across the row. If you are working the edging on a straight edge, make sure to finish with a shell so each end is the same. When working around the entire edge so that you end at the starting point, finish with a single crochet to keep the pattern correct.

4

Picot-shell edging

This is a very pretty lace edging which also can either be worked onto the fabric or sewn on later. Our sample has been worked as a separate edging. You will need a multiple of 6 chains plus 2. For this sample, make 25 chains plus 2 turning chains. Then work single crochet into the chains, beginning with the 3rd chain from hook. Work 26 single crochets, including turning chain.

1 Now work 3 chains and then 2 doubles into the 2nd stitch to make a half shell. Skip the next 5 single crochets and work a complete shell, consisting of 3 doubles, 2 chains and 3 doubles, into the next stitch.

2 Continue to work a shell in this way into every 6th stitch all along the first row, ending by working a half shell of 3 doubles into the top of the turning chain. This first row would make a pretty, but simple, edging on its own.

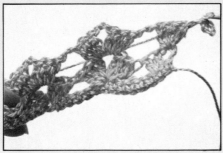

3 To increase the depth of the edging you make more rows of shells. Turn the work and work 3 chains and 2 doubles into the 2nd stitch (middle) of the first half shell. Now work 1 chain, followed by a shell, into the center chain loop of each shell worked in the previous row. Complete the row with a half shell worked into the top of the turning chain.

4 The next row includes the first series of picots. Begin by working 4 chains at the beginning of the row; then work a slip stitch into the first of these 4 chains, thus creating the first picot point.

5 Now work a single crochet into the 2nd stitch (middle) of the first half shell, followed by 3 doubles into the first chain space. Now work the next picot point by working a single crochet, a 4-chain picot point and another single crochet, all into the 2-chain space at the center of the next shell. You have thus made the first picot group, as it will be called from now on.

6 Continue to work 3 doubles into each chain space and a picot group into the center of each shell all the way across the row, ending by working 3 doubles into the last chain space and a single crochet into the turning chain.

7 Now work a picot point in the top of the last stitch in exactly the same way as at the beginning of the row. To hold this last picot firmly, work a slip stitch into the single crochet which you worked into the turning chain.

8 To complete edging work 5 chains to start row, and then work 2 doubles, a picot point and 2 more doubles, all into center of each 3-double crochet group of previous row. This is called a picot shell. Work 2 chains and then work another picot shell into center of next 3-double crochet group. Continue in this way across row. End row by making a picot shell into last 3-double crochet group, then make 2 chains and work a double into top of turning chain to hold group firmly in place.

Mike Berend

Twisted-chain edging

For best results work this unusual edging in two colors. It is worked on a base row of single crochets—a number of stitches divisible by 3. We have called our two colors A and B for ease in following the directions.

1 Using A, work a base row of single crochets on the edge of your fabric, making sure that you have a multiple of 3 stitches. Turn. Still using A, make 4 chains. These 4 chains will count as the first single crochet and 3-chain loop. Skip the next 2 stitches and work a single crochet into the next stitch.

2 Make another 3 chains. Skip the next 2 stitches and work a single crochet into the next stitch. Continue to work a single crochet into every following 3rd stitch, with a 3-chain loop between each stitch all along the row.

3 When you work the last single crochet into the turning chain, join the second color (B) into this stitch by drawing B through the last 2 loops.
Cut off A at this stage. You will need to sew this end to the WS of the fabric once the edging has been completed.

4 Turn. Using B, make 3 chains. Slip the working loop off the hook and hold it in your left hand. Insert the hook under the first loop of the previous row from front to back and through the working loop just made, thus picking up the 3 chains once more.

5 Draw the working loop under the 3-chain loop. Now wind the yarn over the hook and draw it through the loop on the hook to make a slip stitch over the center of the chain loop of the previous row.

6 Now make 3 chains and work 1 single crochet into the same loop as the slip stitch just worked. This makes the first 3-chain loop of the 3rd row of the edging.

7 Repeat steps 4 to 6 all the way along the row until only the last loop of the previous row remains unworked. You will see that the chain loops worked in B appear to have been wound around the chain loops worked in A.

8 When you reach the last loop, work steps 4 to 6 once more into this loop, and then complete the edging by working a slip stitch into the edge of the chain worked in the first loop row to hold the edging firmly in place. Here we show you the edging worked down the side—rather than across—a single crochet fabric.

Mike Berend

Making a simple fringe

Sometimes you may prefer a fringe, instead of a lace edging, as a trimming for your fabric. A fringe is particularly suitable for a very open shawl, which may need the weight of a fringe to show off the stitch pattern. A heavy bedspread will usually look best if edged with a fringe. It is quite simple to work a fringe to any length or thickness you require.

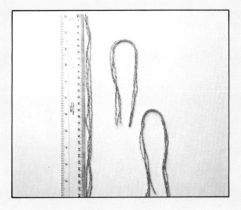

1 Cut at least 3 pieces of yarn, double the length of the finished fringe. The number of lengths will depend on the thickness of the yarn you are using and how thick you want your fringe to be. For this sample we have cut 3 strands of a knitting worsted yarn, 11in (28cm) long for a fringe approximately 5½in (14cm) deep.

2 Now simply knot the groups of 6 strands of yarn into a space on the edge of your fabric. Obviously, if you knot them close together you will obtain a much thicker fringe than if you space them out evenly across the fabric. Finally, trim the bottom of the fringe to make it even.

Gold digger

Create a little excitement with this lacy evening jacket worked in a shell stitch pattern in glittery yarn.

Sizes
To fit 32-36in (83-92cm) bust, approximately.
Length at center back, 23¾in (60cm).

Materials
6oz (150g) of a sport-weight metallic novelty yarn
Size E (3.50mm) crochet hook

Gauge
2 patts and 12 rows to 3½in (9cm) on size E (3.50mm) hook.

To make
Using size E (3.50mm) hook make 106ch and beg at neck edge.
1st row 1dc into 6th ch from hook, *3ch, skip 3ch, 1sc into each of next 3ch, 3ch, skip 3ch, (1dc, 3ch, 1dc) — called V — into next ch, rep from * ending with (1dc, 2ch, 1dc) into last ch. Turn. 10 patts.
2nd row 3ch, 3dc into 2ch sp, *3ch, 1sc into 2nd of 3dc, 3ch, 7dc into 3ch sp of V, rep from * ending with 4dc into sp between first dc and turning ch. Turn.
3rd row 1ch, 1sc into each of next 3dc, *5ch, 1sc into each of next 7dc, rep from * ending with 1sc into each of next 3dc, 1sc into 3rd of 3ch. Turn.
4th row 1ch, 1sc into next sc, *3ch, V into 3rd of 5ch, 3ch, skip 2sc, 1sc into each of next 3sc, rep from * ending 1sc into sc, 1sc into turning ch. Turn.
5th row 4ch, *7dc into 3ch sp of V, 3ch, 1sc into 2nd of 3sc, 3ch, rep from * ending with 7dc into 3ch sp of V, 3ch, 1sc into turning ch. Turn.
6th row 3ch, *1sc into each of next 7dc, 5ch, rep from * ending with 1sc into each of 7dc, 2ch, 1sc into turning ch. Turn.
7th row 5ch to count as first dc and 2ch, 1sc into first sc (edge st), *3ch, skip 2sc, 1sc into each of next 3sc, 3ch, V into 3rd of 5ch, rep from * ending with (1dc, 2ch, 1dc) into turning ch. Turn.
8th row As 2nd.
9th row As 3rd.
10th row 1ch, 1sc into next sc, *3ch, V into 3rd of 5ch, 3ch, skip 2sc, 1sc into each of next 3sc*, 3ch, V into 3rd of 5ch, **3ch, 1sc into first of 7sc, 3ch, V into 4th of 7sc, 3ch, 1sc into 7th of 7sc**, (rep from * to * twice, 3ch, V into 3rd of 5ch, rep from ** to **) twice, rep from * to *, 3ch, V into 3rd of 5ch, 3ch, skip 2sc, 1sc into next sc, 1sc into turning ch. Turn.
11th row 4ch, 7dc into 3ch sp of V, 3ch, 1sc into 2nd of 3sc, 3ch, *(7dc into V, 3ch, 1sc into sc, 3ch) twice, (7dc into V, 3ch, 1sc into 2nd of 3sc, 3ch) twice, rep from * once more, (7dc into V, 3ch, 1sc into sc, 3ch) twice, 7dc into V, 3ch, 1sc into 2nd of 3sc, 3ch, 7dc into V, 3ch, 1sc into turning ch. Turn. 13 patts.
12th row As 6th.
13th row As 7th.
14th row As 2nd.
15th row As 3rd.
16th row 1ch, 1sc into sc, *3ch, V into 3rd of 5ch, 3ch, skip 2sc, 1sc into each of next 3sc*, (3ch, V into 3rd of 5ch, **3ch, 1sc into first of 7sc, 3ch, V into 4th of 7sc, 3ch, 1sc into 7th of 7sc, ** rep from * to * twice) 3 times, 3ch, V into 3rd of 5ch, rep from ** to **, rep from * to *, 3ch, V into 3rd of 5ch, 3ch, skip 2sc, 1sc into next sc, 1sc into turning ch. Turn.
17th row 4ch, 7dc into V, 3ch, 1sc into 2nd of 3sc, *(7dc into V, 3ch, 1sc into sc, 3ch) twice, (7dc into V, 3ch, 1sc into 2nd of 3sc, 3ch) twice, rep from * twice more, (7dc into V, 3ch, 1sc into sc, 3ch) twice, 7dc into V, 3ch, 1sc into 2nd of 3sc, 3ch, 7dc into V, 3ch, 1sc into turning ch. Turn. 17 patts.
18th-21st rows As 12th-15th.
22nd row 1ch, 1sc into next sc, (rep from * to * on 10th row twice, 3ch, V into 3rd of 5ch, rep from ** to ** on 10th row) twice, rep from * to * 4 times, 3ch, V into 3rd of 5ch, rep from ** to **, rep from * to * twice, 3ch, V into 3rd of 5ch, rep from ** to **, rep from * to * twice, 3ch, V into 3rd of 5ch, 3ch, skip 2sc, 1sc into next sc, 1sc into turning ch. Turn.
23rd row As 11th, working 1sc into 2nd of 3sc or into single sc as appropriate. Turn. 21 patts.
24th-27th rows As 12th-15th.
Cont in this way, inc 4 patts on every 6th row, until there are 41 patts. Cont without shaping until work measures approx 15¾in (40cm) from beg.
Divide for sleeves
Next row Work over 6 patts, skip 9 patts, work over 11 patts, skip 9 patts, work over rem 6 patts. Turn.
Cont on these 23 patts until work measures 23¾in (60cm) from beg, ending with a 4th or 7th row. Fasten off.
Edging
Work 1 row sc all around outer edge. Join with sl st to first sc. Turn.
2nd row *5ch, skip 1sc, 1sc into next sc, rep from * all around. Turn.
3rd row Sl st to 3rd ch of first loop, *5ch into 3rd ch of next loop, 1sc into 3rd ch of next loop, rep from * all around.
Work a similar edging around sleeves.
Do not press.

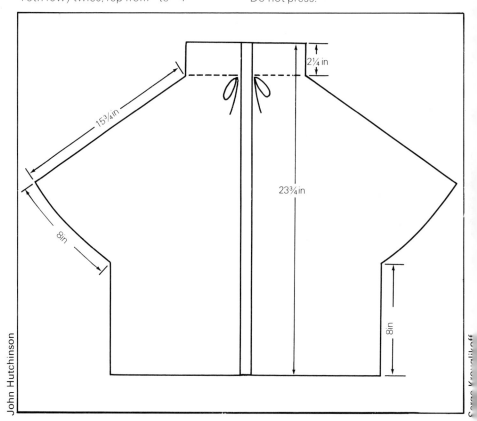

John Hutchinson

Crochet / COURSE 30

*Crocheted buttons
*Covering a round button form
*Buttons filled with cotton

Crocheted buttons

If you want buttons to match the color of a crocheted or knitted garment exactly, why not crochet some? You can work the crochet to cover a button form especially made for this purpose, or you can simply stuff the cover firmly with cotton. Button forms can be bought from most notions departments and craft shops and are available in plastic or metal in a variety of sizes which will suit most requirements.

If the yarn for the main fabric is not too thick, it can also be used for the button; otherwise, it is better to use a matching color in a finer yarn. Crochet cotton and embroidery silk are also suitable, and metallic thread or yarn makes pretty buttons for evening clothes. For an unusual effect, you could even try using shiny raffia. Remember, though, that the yarn or thread you choose must not be so bulky that the completed button can't be passed easily through the buttonhole or loop.

Covering a round button form

A certain amount of trial and error is involved in covering a button form, and it's a good idea to experiment with the form, trying different yarns and methods of working, until the result is satisfactory. For example, if you are covering a small form, you may find it easier to work the cover directly onto it; whereas for a larger form it might be easier to work the cover separately and then slip it on. If you are using a very fine yarn, you may prefer to work in continuous rounds (see Crochet course 15, Volume 4, page 7), rather than joining the ends of each round with a slip stitch as we have done in our sample. On the right are some forms of different sizes. In the top row: plastic forms measuring $\frac{7}{8}$in (22mm) and 1in (25mm) in circumference; below: plastic forms $\frac{3}{4}$in, $1\frac{1}{4}$in and $1\frac{1}{2}$in (19mm, 28mm and 38mm) in diameter.

For our sample we have used sport yarn and a size C (3.00mm) hook for a $1\frac{1}{4}$in (28mm) form (shown on the right with back disk removed). In making a cover you should always use a slightly smaller hook than you would normally use with that yarn for a close, firm fabric.

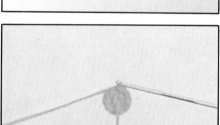

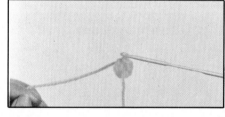

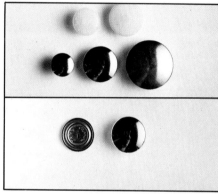

1 Make 3 chains and join them into a circle with a slip stitch. The length of chain you start with should be as short as possible to avoid making a large hole in the center of the cover.

2 Make 1 chain to count as the first single crochet. Now work 5 single crochets into the center of the circle so that you have 6 single crochets in all, including the first chain. Keep the free end of yarn to the front of the work, as this will be the inside of the button. Join the last stitch to the first chain with a slip stitch.

3 Now work 1 chain and then 1 single crochet into the stitch at the base of this chain to begin the next round. Now work 2 single crochets into each stitch all the way around the circle so that you have 12 single crochets in all. Join each round in the same way as in step 2.

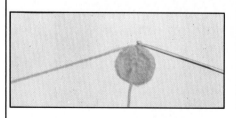

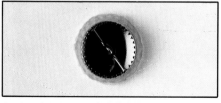

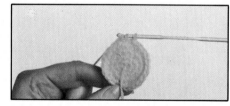

4 To cover the top of a $1\frac{1}{4}$in (28mm) form repeat step 3 once more so that there are 24 stitches in all. Step 3 should be repeated for the size required.

5 Work one round without increasing. Begin with 1 chain, then 1 single crochet into each stitch all around. This round lies at outer edge of the form.

6 Start underside of cover. Make 1 chain. Insert hook into next stitch and draw through a loop twice—3 loops on hook.

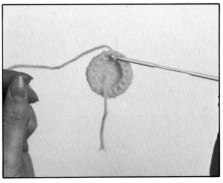

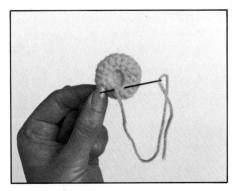

7 Wind the yarn over the hook and draw it through all three loops on the hook. You have thus worked two stitches together to decrease a stitch.

8 Work 1 single crochet into the next stitch, and then work the two following stitches together as before to decrease another stitch. Continue to work a single crochet and then 2 stitches together alternately around the cover, joining the last stitch to the first as before. Eight stitches have been decreased.

9 Work another decrease round in exactly the same way as before. Draw the yarn through and fasten off, leaving a piece of yarn long enough to sew the edges together.

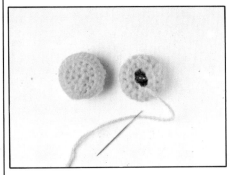

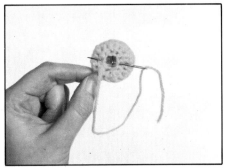

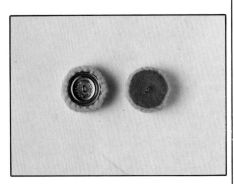

10 Insert the form into the cover, face downward, and adjust the cover so that it fits smoothly and symmetrically over the form.

11 Overcast the edges together as neatly as possible. Make sure that the piece of yarn at the beginning of the round has been secured to the inside of the cover before you begin to sew the edges together.

12 Fasten off the yarn and darn in the loose ends. Attach the back section of the form to the crocheted section. If the thickness of the crochet makes this impossible, you can still neaten the underside of the button by sewing a circle of material onto it.

Buttons filled with cotton

A lighter-weight button can be made by filling the crochet with cotton which is inserted as the crochet is worked. This type of button is ideal for delicate garments.

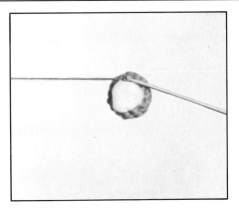

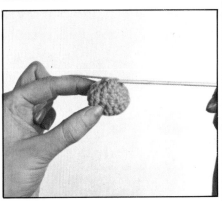

1 To work a small cover over cotton, begin the circle in exactly the same way as for covering a form and increase to shape the fabric. Stuff the cotton firmly into the shape as you work.

2 Complete the button by decreasing in the same way as for covering a form, until the circle is almost closed. Then work a slip stitch through the edges, before drawing the yarn through the working loop to fasten it off and complete the cover.

Fred Mancini

*Shell-fabric pattern
*Eyelet-lace pattern
*Pattern for woman's shirt-
 style sweater and girl's tunic

Shell-fabric pattern

This very simple shell stitch pattern has been used for the woman's shirt and the girl's tunic featured in this course. It has a slightly textured appearance without being too bulky. Because the pattern consists of two stitches worked into one, making a fan-shaped group, it is important to work the foundation chain as loosely as possible.

Before making one of the garments in this course, make a sample to check your gauge and see the overall effect. If necessary, work the foundation chains with a larger hook than the one used for the pattern.

As you can see from the girl's tunic, it is possible to work bands of color by introducing new colors at the end of a row. We worked one row in the first contrasting color, followed by three rows in a second contrasting color. The pattern is worked over an even number of stitches. We have made 25 chains and worked the first single crochet into the 3rd chain from the hook, so that there are 24 single crochets in the first row of the sample.

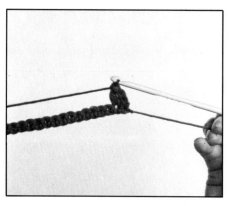

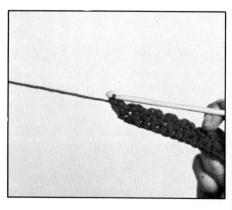

1 On the first row of the pattern you will not need to work any turning chains, since the first shell group is worked at the edge of the fabric. Begin by working a single crochet, chain and double crochet all into the 2nd stitch to form the first graduated shell.

2 Now skip the next single crochet and work another group into the next stitch. Continue to work a group in the same way into every other stitch all the way across the row, working the last group into the top of the turning chain to complete the row.

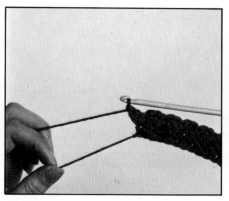

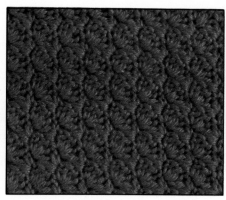

3 Now turn the work and make 2 chains. From this point on, a turning chain is required at the beginning of every row. Skip the first double crochet and 1-chain space and work a group in the same way as before the next single crochet. (This is the single crochet worked at the beginning of the last group in the previous row.)

4 Continue to work a group in the same way into each single crochet worked in the previous row until you reach the end of the row. The last group should be worked into the edge of the fabric this time, since there is no turning chain.

5 To continue the pattern, repeat the 2nd row each time, remembering that the last group should be worked into the top of the turning chain on subsequent rows.

Eyelet-lace pattern

This fabric has a slightly lacy look and could be used for a summer blouse or an evening top. The pattern is worked over a multiple of 6 chains plus 3 extra. Our sample requires 27 chains in all, and is worked in a knitting worsted yarn with a size G (4.50mm) hook, although this pattern looks equally good worked in a finer ply yarn or cotton yarn.

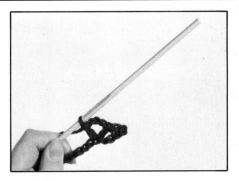

1 Work a single crochet into the 3rd chain from the hook. Now skip the next 2 chains and work 1 double, followed by 3 chains and 1 double, all into the next chain to create the first V-shaped group. Now skip the next 2 chains and work a single crochet into the following chain.

2 Continue to work a V group and a single crochet alternately across the row into every 3rd chain, completing the row by working a single crochet into the last chain. The pattern consists of these two simple steps worked alternately, reversing their position on every row.

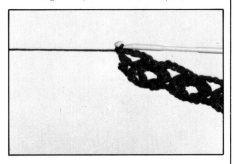

3 To keep the edge of the fabric straight and the pattern running in the correct sequence, you will have to work a half V at the beginning of the next row. This is done by working 4 chains to count as first double and 1 chain, then 1 double into first stitch to complete group. The half group is achieved by working 1 chain between the 2 doubles.

4 Now work a single crochet into the next 3-chain loop at the center of the first V group, followed by a V group into the single crochet between the first two V groups worked in the previous row.

5 Continue to work a single crochet and a V group alternately across the row, completing the row by working a half V group consisting of 1 double, 1 chain and 1 double all worked into the top of the turning chain.

6 Begin the next row with 1 chain and then work a single crochet into the chain space in the center of the first half V group at the edge of the work.

7 Now work a V group as before into the single crochet between the first and 2nd V groups in the previous row, thus reversing the pattern once more. Continue to work a V group and single crochet alternately across the row, finishing by working a single crochet into the 3rd of the first 4 chain, thus leaving the 4th of these chain to count as the 1-chain space in the V group of the previous row.

8 The overall eyelet effect is created by alternating rows in this way for the pattern, beginning one row with a half V group and the next with a single crochet.

Fred Mancini

Mother and daughter duo

A beautifully casual pair for mother and daughter, worked in a shell-stitch fabric and trimmed with crochet-covered buttons. The girl's tunic follows the lines of the shirt-style sweater, but has bands of color across the shoulders.

Victor Yuan

Woman's shirt

Sizes
To fit 34[36:38]in (87[92:97]cm) bust. Length, 25¼[26:26¾]in (64[66:68]cm). Sleeve seam, 17[17¼:17¾]in (43[44:45]cm).
Note Directions for larger sizes are in brackets []; if there is only one set of figures it applies to all sizes.

Materials
16[18:20]oz (450[500:550]g) of a sport yarn
Sizes C and E (3.00 and 3.50mm) crochet hooks
Cotton for buttons

Gauge
7½ groups and 18 rows to 4in (10cm) on size E (3.50mm) hook.

Back
Using size E (3.50mm) hook make 80[84:88] ch very loosely.
Base row 1 sc into 3rd ch from hook, 1 sc into each ch to end. 79[83:87] sts. Cut off yarn and turn.
Shape lower edge
1st row Skip 24sc, rejoin yarn to next sc, 1ch, (1sc, 1ch, 1dc) into next sc—called 1 group or 1 grp—, (skip next sc, 1 grp into next sc) 14[16:18] times, 1sc into next sc, turn (leaving 24 sts unused at end).
2nd row 2ch, skip first sc, (1grp into sc of next grp) 15[17:19] times, sl st into 1ch at beg of first row, (skip next sc, 1 grp into next sc) twice, 1sc into next sc, turn (thus using 5 of the sc which were left at beg of first row).
3rd row 2ch, skip first sc, (1grp into sc of next grp) 17[19:21] times, sl st into 2ch at beg of last row, (skip next sc, 1 grp into next sc) twice, 1sc into next sc, turn. Working 2 more grp on each row, rep the 3rd row 6 times more.
10th row 2ch, skip first sc, (1grp into sc of next grp) 31[33:35] times, sl st into 2ch at beg of last row, (skip next sc, 1grp into next sc) twice, turn.
11th row 1ch, (1 grp into sc of next grp) 33[35:37] times, sl st into 2ch at beg of last row, (skip next sc, 1grp into next sc) twice, turn. 35[37:39] grp.
All sc left unused at beg are now used up, as you used 5sc at end of every row until last 2 rows and 4 at end of last 2 rows.
12th row 1ch, 1grp into sc of each grp. Rep 12th row until work measures 17¾in (45cm) (measured at center).
Shape armholes
Next row Sl st over 2grp, 1ch, patt to within last 2grp, turn.
Next row Patt to end. Turn.
Next row Sl st over first grp, 1ch, patt to within last grp, turn.
Rep last 2 rows twice more. 25[27:29] grp. Cont straight until armholes measure 7½[8¼:9]in (19[21:23]cm).

Shape shoulders
Next row Sl st over 2grp, patt to within last 2grp, turn.
Next row Sl st over 2[3:3]grp, patt to within last 2[3:3]grp, turn.
Next row Sl st over 3grp, patt to within last 3grp. Fasten off.

Front
Work as for back until work measures 13¾in (35cm) from beg.
Divide for front opening
Next row Work 17[18:19]grp, turn and cont on these sts until work measures same as back to armholes, ending at side.
Shape armhole
Next row Sl st over 2grp, 1ch, patt to end. Turn.
Next row Patt to end. Turn.
Next row Sl st over first grp, patt to end. Rep last 2 rows twice more. 12[13:14] grp. Cont straight until armhole measures 5½[6¼:7]in (14[16:18]cm); end at armhole edge.
Shape neck
Next row Patt to within last 2[2:3]grp, turn.
Next row Patt to end. Turn.
Next row Patt to within last grp, turn. Rep last 2 rows twice. Work rem 7[8:8] grp until armhole is same as back; end at armhole edge.
Shape shoulder
Next row Sl st over 2grp, patt to end. Turn.
Next row Patt to last 2[2:3]grp, turn.
Next row Sl st over 3grp, patt to end. Fasten off. Return to where work was left, rejoin yarn to next sc, 1ch, 1grp into next sc, patt to end. Turn. 17[18:19]grp. Complete to match first side, reversing shaping.

Sleeves
Using size E (3.50mm) hook make 51[55:59]ch.
Base row 1sc into 3rd ch from hook, 1sc into each ch to end. Turn. 50[54:58] sts.
1st row 1ch, skip first sc, 1grp into next sc, *skip next sc, 1grp into next sc, rep from * to end. Turn. 25[27:29]grp.
2nd row 1ch, 1grp into sc of each grp to end. Rep 2nd row until work measures 17[17¼:17¾]in (43[44:45]cm) from beg.
Shape top
Next row Sl st over first grp, 1ch, patt to last 2grp, turn. Rep last row 7[8:9] times more.
Fasten off.

Cuffs (make 2)
Using size C (3.00mm) hook make 7ch.
Base row 1sc into 3rd ch from hook, 1sc into each ch to end. Turn. 6 sts.
Next row 2ch to count as first sc, 1sc into each sc to end. Turn.
Rep last row for 7[7½:7¾]in (18[19:20]cm).
Fasten off.

Collar
Using size C (3.00mm) hook make 13ch and work base row as for cuffs. 12sc. Cont in sc for 14¼[15:15¾]in (36[38:40]cm).
Fasten off.

To finish
Do not press. Join shoulders. Sew in sleeves, sewing last ¾in (2cm) of sleeve seams to first 2grp of armhole. Seam sides and sleeves, leaving sleeve seams open for about 2¾in (7cm) from lower edge. Sew on cuffs, gathering sleeve edge to fit. Sew on collar.

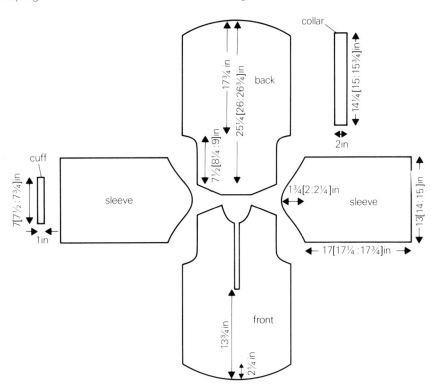

Brian Mayor

Front fastening

Beg at top of left front collar, work 1 row of sc around opening. Turn. Work another row of sc, making eight 5-chain button loops, first at neck edge and 7 evenly spaced down right front.
Make eight buttons (see page 11) and sew to left front.

Tunic

Victor Yuan

Brian Mayor

Sizes

To fit 22[24:26]in (56[61:66]cm) chest.
Length, 18¼[20:22¼]in (46[51:56]cm).
Sleeve, 8¾[9½:10¼]in (22[24:26]cm).

Note Directions for larger sizes are in brackets []; if there is only one set of figures it applies to all sizes.

Materials

8[8:9]oz (200[200:250]g) of a sport yarn in main color (A)
2oz (50g) in each of 2 contrasting colors (B and C)
Sizes C and E (3.00 and 3.50mm) crochet hooks
Cotton for buttons

Gauge

7½ groups and 18 rows to 4in (10cm) on size E (3.50mm) hook.

Back

Using size E (3.50mm) hook and A, make 51[55:59]ch.
Base row. 1sc into 3rd ch from hook, 1sc into each ch to end. Turn.
1st row 1ch, skip first sc, (1sc, 1ch and 1dc) into next sc—called 1 group or 1 grp, *skip next sc, 1grp into next sc, rep from * to end. Turn. 25[27:29]grp.
2nd row 1ch, 1grp into sc of each grp to end.
Rep the 2nd row until work measures 13[14½:16¼]in (33[37:41]cm).
Shape armholes
Next row Sl st over 2grp, 1ch, patt to within last 2grp, turn.
Next row Patt to end. Turn.
Next row Sl st over first grp, 1ch, patt to within last grp, turn.
Rep last 2 rows once. Work 1[3:5] rows straight. Cut off A. Join on B and work 2 rows. Join on C and work 6 rows. With B work 2 rows. Cut off B. Cont with C until armholes measure 5¼[5½:6]in (13[14:15]cm).
Fasten off.

Front

Work as for back until work measures 11[12½:14¼]in (28[32:36]cm).
Divide for front opening
Next row Patt over 12[13:14]grp, turn. Cont on these sts until work measures same as back to armhole; end at side edge.
Shape armhole
Next row Sl st over 2grp, 1ch, patt to end. Turn.
Next row Patt to end. Turn.
Next row Sl st over first grp, 1ch, patt to end. Turn. Rep last 2 rows once. Work 1[3:5] rows straight. Cont in stripes to match back until armhole measures 3½[4:4¼]in (9[10:11]cm); end at armhole edge.
Shape neck
Next row Patt to within last 2grp, turn.
Next row Patt to end. Turn.
Next row Patt to within last grp, turn.
For 3rd size only, rep last 2 rows once. For all sizes, cont straight until armhole measures same as back. Fasten off. Return to where sts were left, rejoin yarn to next sc, 1ch, 1grp into next sc, patt to end. Turn. Complete to match first side, reversing shaping.

Sleeves

Using size E (3.50mm) hook and A, make 31[35:39]ch. Work base row as for back. 15[17:19] grp. Cont in patt as for back until sleeve measures 8¾[9½:10¼]in (22[24:26]cm).
Shape top
Next row Sl st over first grp, 1ch, patt to within last grp, turn.
Rep this row 4[5:6] times.
Fasten off.

Cuffs

Using size C (3.00mm) hook and B, make 6ch.
Base row 1sc into 3rd ch from hook, 1sc into each ch to end. Turn. 5sts.
Next row 2ch to count as first sc, 1sc into each sc to end. Turn. Rep last row until cuff measures 6[6¼:6¾]in (15[16:17]cm).
Fasten off.

Collar

Using size C (3.00mm) hook and B, make 11ch and work base row as for cuffs. 10sc. Cont in sc for 10¼[11:11¾]in (26[28:30]cm).
Fasten off.

To finish

Finish as for woman's shirt.

Front fastening

Using B, work front edging as for woman's shirt, making six 5-chain button loops on right front.
With C, make six small buttons (see page 11) and sew to left front.

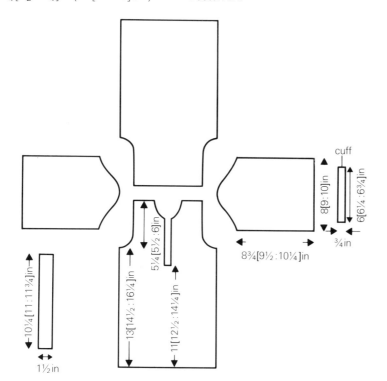

cuff
8[9:10]in
6[6¼:6¾]in
¾in
8¾[9½:10¼]in
10¼[11:11¾]in
13[14½:16¼]in
5¼[5½:6]in
11[12½:14¼]in
1½in

Crochet / COURSE 32

Introduction to filet crochet

Filet crochet is really a simple form of lace, the name being taken from the French word meaning "net." It was originally inspired by filet guipure lace which, in its turn, was derived from the medieval craft of darning delicate flower patterns onto handmade net backgrounds. Filet crochet was very popular in the second half of the nineteenth century throughout America, where it was used extensively to decorate any number of household items with monograms, simple sayings, or a variety of different flower patterns and motifs. Sheets, pillowcases, tablecloths, mats, towels and baby linen were often trimmed with filet edgings or insertions.

Traditionally, filet crochet is worked in fine white or ecru cotton thread, using a very small hook, and today these fine threads are available in a great variety of colors. But filet patterns are no longer confined to delicate trimmings and edgings. Worked in thicker cottons or knitting yarns, filet crochet can be used to create an entire fabric with a beautiful, lacy look, suitable for clothing and household items.

Making the basic filet mesh

The basic mesh is made by working single doubles with either 1 or 2 chains worked between the doubles (depending on the thickness of the yarn being used) to form the spaces of the mesh. When working with a fine crochet cotton and hook it is important to make sure that you work as neatly as possible, so that the resulting fabric is really firm and even. You can either make the mesh in a fine crochet cotton for a really light, lacy fabric, or try it in a thick crochet cotton or knitting yarn for a more solid-looking fabric.

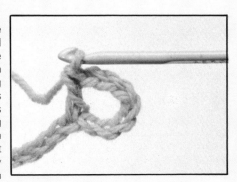

1 Make 32 chains and then work a double into the 8th chain from the hook. These first 7 chains will count as the first double (3 chains) and the 2-chain space on the foundation chain and on the first row.

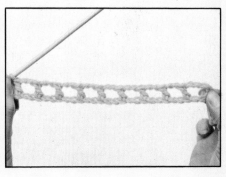

2 Now make 2 chains, skip the next 2 chains in the base chain and work another double into the next chain, so that you have worked the 2nd space of the mesh. Continue this way across the chain, working the last double into the last chain. You should have 9 spaces in all.

3 On the next row begin by working 5 chains. These will count as the first double (3 chains) and the first 2-chain space. Skip the next 2 chains and work a double into the next double in the previous row.

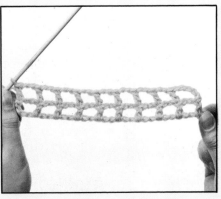

4 Continue to work in the same way all the way across so that you finish with 9 spaces as before. Work the last double into the 3rd of the 7 chains.

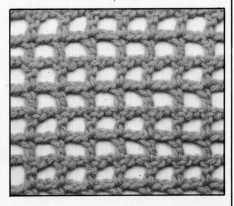

5 To continue working the mesh, repeat the 2nd row each time. You should work the last double into the 3rd of the first 5 chains at the end of every row, so that 2 chains will count as the last space at the end of the row.

Mike Berend

Working the double crochet blocks

To make filet patterns, the spaces of the mesh must be filled with blocks of doubles. Each block is made by working 2 doubles into any of the spaces in the basic mesh, with a double worked into the double on each side of the space so that the completed block will consist of 4 doubles in all. You can work alternate blocks and spaces across the row, changing the position of each on the following row for a simple checkerboard pattern. Or, by working two or three blocks side by side, you can make a more intricate pattern. Try working a narrow strip of blocks and spaces in a fine crochet cotton as a simple edging for a placemat.

The basic working method is always the same whether the filet pattern is simple or complicated.

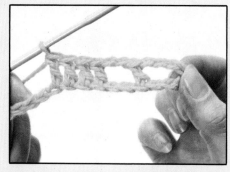

1 Make 38 chains and begin the row in the same way as for the plain filet mesh, making 2 spaces at the beginning of the chain. Now work 1 double into each of the next 3 chains, thus creating the first block of 4 doubles. (The double after 2nd space counts as first double of block.)

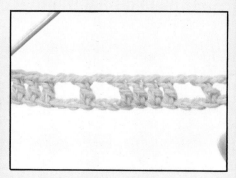

2 Make 2 more spaces in the same way as for the filet mesh, then another block of doubles in the same way as before over the next 3 chains.

6 Make 2 chains, skip the next 2 doubles in the block in the row below and work 1 double into the next double, so that you have worked a space over the block in the previous row.

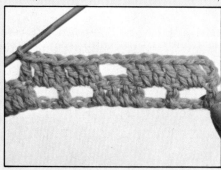

7 Now work 2 more blocks in the same way as before over the next 2 spaces so that you work 7 doubles in all.

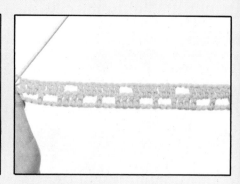

8 Continue to work a space over each block and a block into each space worked in the previous row, ending by working 2 blocks together at the end of the row. The last double of the last block should be worked into the top of the turning chain.

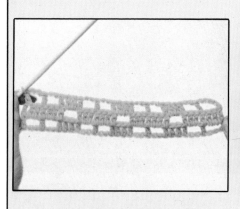

12 Work 2 more spaces as before over the next 2 blocks and then a block into the next space. Continue to work 2 spaces over the blocks and a block into each space all the way across the row, so that you finish the row with 2 spaces. Work the last double into the top of the turning chain.

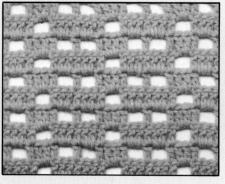

13 Continue the pattern by working alternate rows of 2 spaces and 1 block and then 2 blocks and 1 space to make the overall checked pattern.

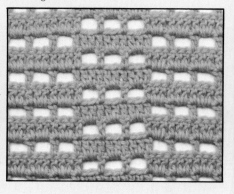

14 When you work 3 blocks together you should have 10 doubles in all to complete the 3 blocks. In the same way, when working 4 blocks side by side, you will work 13 doubles in all. The reason is that although each block worked by itself consists of 4 doubles, when two or more blocks are worked side by side, the last double of one block also counts as the first double of the next block.

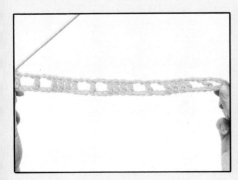 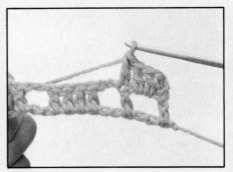 

3 Repeat step 2 once more and then make 2 more spaces to complete the row. You should have 3 blocks of doubles with 2 spaces worked between each block.

4 Begin the next row by making 3 chains to count as the first double. Now work 2 doubles into the first space and a double into the next double to make the first block into the first space.

5 Now work 2 doubles into the next space and a double into the next double (the first double of the first block in the previous row). Thus you have worked 2 blocks together. You will see that the 2 blocks consist of 7 doubles in all.

9 On the next row begin by making 5 chains. These chains will count as the first double and 2-chain space. Skip the first 3 doubles (including the edge stitch) and work a double into the 4th double to create the first space in this row.

10 Make 2 chains. Skip the next 2 doubles in the row below and work a double into the next double, thus making the 2nd space.

11 Now work 2 doubles into the next space of the previous row and a double into the first double in the next block to make the first block of 4 doubles in this row.

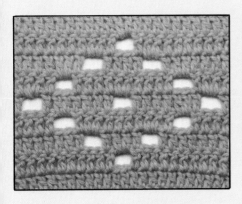  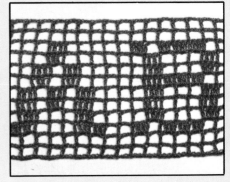

15 This sample shows a piece of filet crochet worked in a knitting worsted, with spaces worked on a solid double background to create the central diamond pattern. This pattern would be just as effective worked in a cotton yarn.

16 The same pattern, except that blocks have been worked instead of the spaces and spaces instead of blocks, to create a much more open, lacy effect.

17 A sample of traditional filet crochet worked in a medium-weight crochet cotton where the letters A and B have been worked onto a mesh background, using blocks to create the letters.

Mike Berend

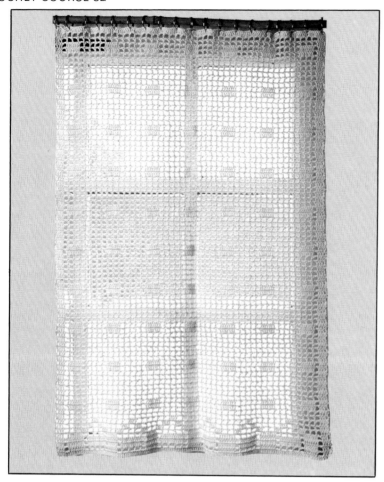

Kim Sayer

The light touch

This delicate curtain, worked in a very simple filet pattern, provides a pretty and decorative screen.

Size
21in (53cm) by 31in (79cm).

Materials
9oz (250g) of a lightweight mercerized crochet cotton
Size B (2.50mm) crochet hook
19 1in (2.5cm) curtain rings

Gauge
9 blocks or sp and 11 rows to 4in (10cm).

Note 1 block consists of 4dc with 3dc for each additional block worked alongside.

To make
Using size B (2.50mm) hook make 147ch loosely.
1st row 1dc into 4th ch from hook, 1dc into each ch to end. Turn. 145 sts.
2nd row 3ch to count as first dc, 1dc into each of next 3dc—1 block formed or 1 blk, 2ch, skip next 2dc, 1dc into next dc —1 space formed or 1sp, 1dc into each of next 6dc—2blks formed, *(2ch, skip next 2dc, 1dc into next dc) 5 times—5sp formed, 1dc into each of next 6dc— 2blks formed, rep from * 5 times more, 2ch, skip next 2dc, 1dc into next dc—1sp

formed, 1dc into each of next 2dc, 1dc into top of the 3ch. Turn.
3rd row 1blk, 1sp, 2blks, *1sp, 3blks, 1sp, 2blks, rep from * 5 times more, 1sp, 1blk. Turn.
4th row As 3rd row.
5th row 1blk, 1sp, 2blks, *5sp, 2blks, rep from * 5 times more, 1sp, 1blk. Turn.
6th row 1blk, 3sp, *1blk, 3sp, 1blk, 2sp, rep from * 5 times more, 1sp, 1blk. Turn.
7th row 1blk, 4sp, *1blk, 1sp, 1blk, 4sp, rep from * 5 times more, 1blk. Turn.
8th row 1blk, 5sp, *1blk, 6sp, rep from * 4 times more, 1blk, 5sp, 1blk. Turn.
9th row 1blk, 46sp, 1blk. Turn.
10th row As 9th row.
11th row 1blk, 1sp, *2blks, 5sp, rep from * 5 times more, 2blks, 1sp, 1blk. Turn.
12th row As 11th row.
13th-18th rows Rep 9th row 6 times.
19th and 20th rows As 11th row.
Rep the 13th-20th rows 8 times more, then the 9th row twice.
87th row 3ch, 1dc into each of next 3dc, *2dc into sp, 1dc into next dc, rep from * to within last blk, 1dc into each of next 2dc, 1dc into top of 3ch. Fasten off. Press. Attach rings to top edge.

Tea-time special

Add a touch of elegance to an informal table setting. These placemats with a matching runner have a pretty diamond pattern.

Placemats

Size
8¾in (22cm) by 11¾in (30cm).

Materials
2oz (50g) of a medium-weight crochet cotton will make one mat
Size F (4.00mm) crochet hook

Gauge
7sp to 3¼in (8cm).

Note 1 block consists of 3dc with 2dc for each additional block worked alongside.

To make
Using size F (4.00mm) hook make 57ch.
1st row 1dc into 4th ch from hook, 1dc into each ch to end. Turn. 55sts.
2nd row 3ch to count as first dc, 1dc into each of next 8dc—4 blocks formed or 4blks, (1ch, skip next dc, 1dc into next dc) 19 times—19 spaces formed or 19sp, 1dc into each of next 7dc, 1dc into top of the 3ch—4blks formed. Turn.
3rd row 3blks, 10sp, 1blk, 10sp, 3blks. Turn.
4th row 2blks, 10sp, 3blks, 10sp, 2blks. Turn.
5th row 1blk, 10sp, 5blks, 10sp, 1blk. Turn.
6th row 1blk, 9sp, 7blks, 9sp, 1blk. Turn.
7th row 1blk, 7sp, 1blk, 2sp, 5blks, 2sp, 1blk, 7sp, 1blk. Turn.
8th row 1blk, 6sp, 3blks, 2sp, 3blks, 2sp, 3blks, 6sp, 1blk. Turn.
9th row 1blk, 5sp, 5blks, 2sp, 1blk, 2sp, 5blks, 5sp, 1blk. Turn.
10th row 1blk, 4sp, 17blks, 4sp, 1blk. Turn.
11th-17th rows Work 9th-3rd rows in this order.
18th row 4blks, 19sp, 4blks. Turn.
19th row 3ch, 1dc into each of next 8dc, (1dc into next sp, 1dc into next dc) 19 times, 1dc into each of last 8dc. Fasten off. Press work lightly on the wrong side with a warm iron over a damp cloth.

Table runner

Size
9½in (24cm) by 37in (94cm).

Materials
6oz (150g) of a medium-weight crochet cotton
Size F (4.00mm) crochet hook

Gauge

7 sp to 3¼in (8cm).

Note 1 block consists of 3dc, with 2dc for each additional block that is worked alongside it.

To make

Using size F (4.00mm) hook make 49ch.

1st row 1dc into 4th ch from hook, 1dc into each ch to end. Turn. 47sts.

2nd row 3ch to count as first dc, 1dc into each of next 8dc—4 blocks formed or 4blks, (1ch, skip next dc, 1dc into next dc) 15 times—15 spaces formed or 15sp, 1dc into each of next 7dc, 1dc into top of the 3ch—4blks formed.

Turn.

3rd row 3blks, 8sp, 1blk, 8sp, 3blks. Turn.

4th row 2blks, 8sp, 3blks, 8sp, 2blks. Turn.

5th row 1blk, 8sp, 5blks, 8sp, 1blk. Turn.

6th row 1blk, 7sp, 7blks, 7sp, 1blk. Turn.

7th row 1blk, 5sp, 1blk, 2sp, 5blks, 2sp, 1blk, 5sp, 1blk. Turn.

8th row 1blk, 4sp, 3blks, 2sp, 3blks, 2sp, 3blks, 4sp, 1blk. Turn.

9th row 1blk, 3sp, 5blks, 2sp, 1blk, 2sp, 5blks, 3sp, 1blk. Turn.

10th row 1blk, 2sp, 17blks, 2sp, 1blk. Turn.

11th-15th rows Work 9th-5th rows in this order.

16th row 1blk, 9sp, 3blks, 9sp, 1blk. Turn.

17th row 1blk, 10sp, 1blk, 10sp, 1blk. Turn.

18th row 1blk, 21sp, 1blk. Turn.

19th row 1blk, 10sp, 1blk, 10sp, 1blk. Turn.

20th row 1blk, 9sp, 3blks, 9sp, 1blk. Turn.

21st row 1blk, 8sp, 5blks, 8sp, 1blk. Turn.

Rep 6th-21st rows 3 times more, then work 6th-15th rows again.

Next row As 4th row.

Next row As 3rd row.

Next row 4blks, 15sp, 4blks. Turn.

Next row 3ch, 1dc into each of next 8dc, (1dc into next sp, 1dc into next dc) 15 times, 1dc into each of last 8dc.

Fasten off. Press work lightly on WS as for placemats.

Kim Sayer

21

Crochet / COURSE 33

*Filet mesh variations
*Using filet charts
*How to make your own
  chart
*Pattern for a short-sleeved
  top

Filet mesh variations

In Crochet course 32 we showed you how to make the basic filet mesh using 2 chains with a double worked at each side to form the spaces. It is sometimes necessary to vary the size of the mesh, either to suit the yarn you are working with, or to obtain a smaller or larger mesh for the pattern you are making.

Here are two examples of variations on the basic mesh, one for a finer mesh, one for a more widely spaced mesh.

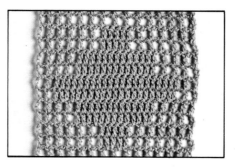

Fine crochet cotton mesh

In this case you will work only 1 double into the spaces to form the blocks, rather than 2, so that each block will consist of a total of 3 doubles in all. Thus to work the blocks side by side you should work an extra 2 doubles each time so that two blocks will consist of 5 doubles, three blocks of 7 doubles and so on.

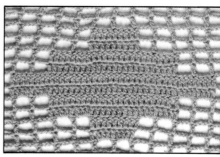

Thick yarn mesh

Similarly when working with a thicker cotton yarn or knitting yarn, or to make a more widely spaced mesh, work 3 chains between each double to form the spaces each time. In this case you will work 3 doubles into each space to form the blocks so they will consist of 5 doubles. To work 2 or more blocks side by side you'll need to work a further 4 doubles each time so you should work 9 doubles for 2 consecutive blocks and so on.

Using filet charts

Because many of the patterns used for filet crochet are so intricate and detailed, it would be far too lengthy and complicated to write the patterns in row by row directions in the normal way. For this reason they are usually set out in the form of a chart on graph paper, each horizontal square representing a space or block and each vertical square representing a row. A symbol, for example X, is used to represent each block in the pattern, the spaces being shown as a blank square for clarity, so that you can immediately see how many blocks and spaces should be worked on each row to complete the pattern.

Because of the depth of the basic stitch (double) used in filet patterns it is difficult to work motifs with very detailed and intricate outlines. Nevertheless, there are still a great many traditional patterns which can be worked, such as roses or simple animal shapes, or more intricate patterns like bunches or baskets of

flowers, which are usually worked in fine crochet cotton. Geometric designs are also used, especially when a larger pattern is needed for something like a bedspread. Once you have mastered the basic technique as shown in our step-by-step instructions you will be able to follow filet charts and even work out your own designs.

The very simple butterfly motif featured on the front of the filet crochet top on page 26 would take many rows of complicated directions if written out in the conventional form used for normal crochet patterns.

Here the motif has been drawn onto graph paper in the form of a chart, so that you can see at a glance how the complete motif is worked. Each square is represented by a blank square and each block by an X on the chart. The uneven rows (RS of work) are numbered vertically on the right-hand side of the chart and will be read from right to left. The even rows (WS of work) will be read from left to right.

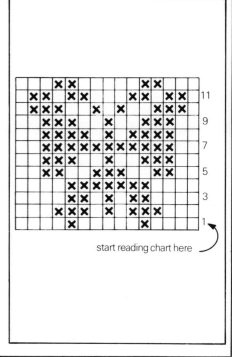

start reading chart here

Working from the chart

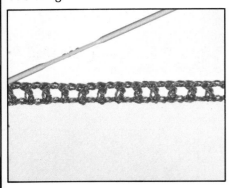

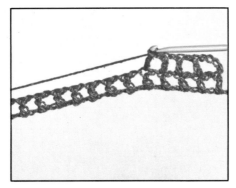

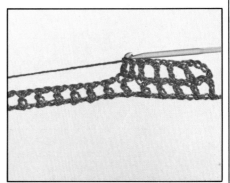

1 To make this motif make 34 chains and then work 1 double into 6th chain from the hook to make the first space. Continue to work across the row by making 1 chain, skipping a chain and working 1 double into the following chain for each space so that you have 15 spaces in all at the end of the row.

2 Now begin to work from the chart. Start to work the first row from the right-hand side of the chart as shown, reading this row from right to left. Make 4 chains to count as the first double and chain on this and every row and then work 4 spaces over the first 4 spaces in the previous row, making them in exactly the same way as before.

3 Now make the first block by working 1 double into the next space and a double into the next double. Thus the block consists of 3 doubles in all, the last double of the last space counting as the first double of the block. To work 2 or more blocks side by side work an additional 2 doubles each time, so that 2 blocks consist of 5 doubles, 3 of 7 doubles and so on.

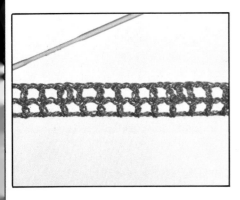

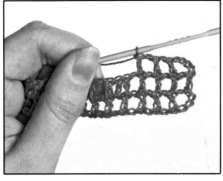

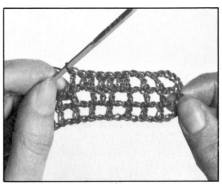

4 Now continue to work across the row reading the chart from right to left and working each space and block as shown on the chart. The last double of the last space should always be worked into the 3rd chain of the turning chain.

5 Now turn the work and begin to work the 2nd row of the pattern from the chart, working the row from left to right this time. This row will be on the WS of the work. Work all even rows from left to right in the same way. Begin by making 4 chains and then work 3 spaces over the 3 spaces in the previous row.

6 Now work 3 consecutive blocks, so that you work 7 doubles in all (a double into each space and a double into each double over the next 2 spaces and 1 block in the previous row).

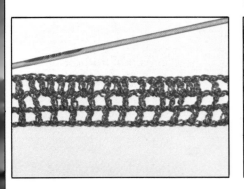

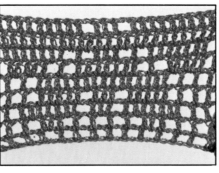

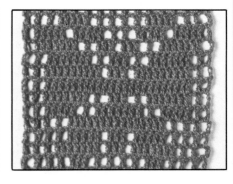

7 Complete the row working the spaces and blocks exactly as shown in the chart and continuing to read the row from left to right.

8 Now turn and continue to work the motif from the chart in the same way remembering to work each uneven row from right to left and each even row from left to right.

9 Complete the motif by working a row of spaces at the top of the fabric after the last row of the chart has been worked to match the spaces worked at the bottom of the fabric.

Fred Mancini

How to repeat a pattern on a filet chart

Sometimes your pattern may require you to repeat a motif several times across the row. The chart will be set out in exactly the same way as for a single motif, except that the blocks and spaces to be worked consecutively across the row will be shown between either a bracket or vertical lines marked clearly on the chart; this will be known as the pattern repeat. The stitches marked at each end of the chart on each side of the pattern repeat are the edge stitches of the pattern and should only be worked at the beginning or end of the row, depending on whether you are working the RS or WS rows. For example the edge stitches on the right-hand side of this chart will be worked at the beginning of the uneven rows and at the end of even rows.

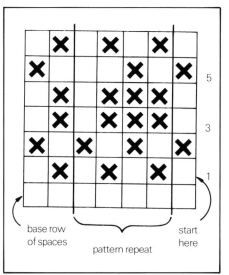

base row of spaces

pattern repeat

start here

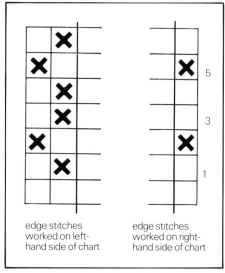

edge stitches worked on left-hand side of chart

edge stitches worked on right-hand side of chart

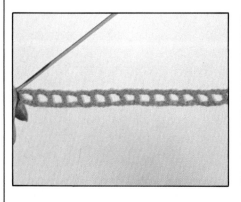

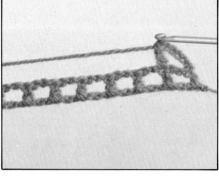

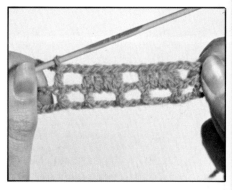

1 To make this sample you will need to start with a multiple of 4 spaces (pattern repeat), plus 3 extra spaces for the edges. We have made 15 spaces (with 2 chains worked between each double to form the spaces) in all, so that the pattern will be repeated 3 times.

2 Start working the chart from the bottom right-hand corner as before, reading row 1 from right to left, working the first space at the beginning of the row.

3 Now work the spaces and blocks for the first pattern repeat shown in the bracket, reading the chart from right to left as before (each block should consist of 4 doubles as shown in Basic filet mesh page 18). Do not work the edge stitches shown after the bracket on the left-hand side of the chart.

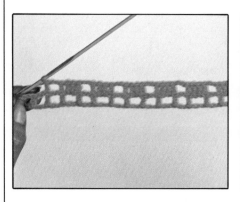

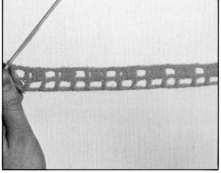

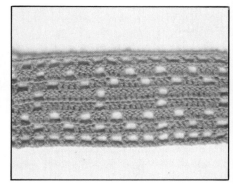

4 Continue to work the pattern repeat, reading from right to left until only 2 spaces remain unworked at the edge of the fabric.

5 Now complete the row by working the last block and space at the edge of the chart. These stitches count as the end of the first row on the RS and the beginning of the 2nd row on the WS.

6 Continue to work from the chart until the pattern is complete, working each row exactly the same way, so that for this sample the pattern will be repeated 3 times in each row. Remember to work each RS (uneven) row from right to left and each WS (even) row from left to right.

How to make your own chart

Now that you've learned how to read and work from a filet crochet chart you should find it easy to design your own patterns using the same basic working method. Embroidery motifs and patterns as well as some colorwork knitting designs can easily be adapted into filet charts, provided that the outline of the motif is not too intricate. Because of the depth of the spaces and blocks it is difficult to achieve detailed outlines on a motif if you are using a widely spaced mesh on a small area, such as a place mat. In this case it would be better to stick to simple geometric patterns. However, you will be able to achieve quite intricate outlines when working with a fine yarn and hook over a fairly large area on something like a large tablecloth.

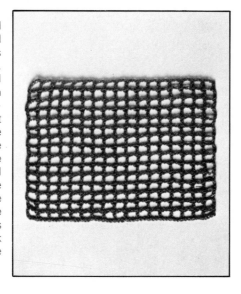

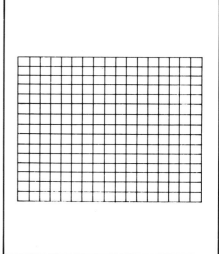

1 Begin by making a gauge sample in the yarn and mesh of your choice, so that you can measure how many spaces and rows there are to a specific measurement—1in or 2in (2.5cm or 5cm) is best. Thus you will be able to work out the size of your motif or pattern once it has been drawn onto your grid. The proportions may vary with your gauge.

2 Draw a grid on plain paper, using a fine pen. Start by drawing a rectangle the same size as your gauge sample. Then divide it up as accurately as possible into the same number of rectangular spaces and rows as the sample.

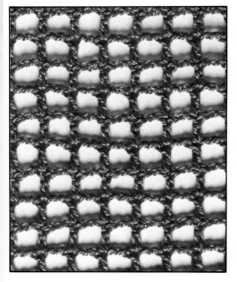

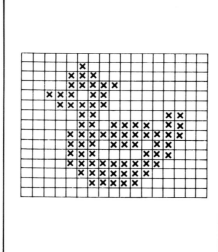

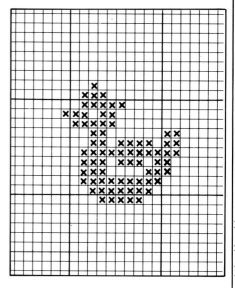

3 You will see that the spaces are not completely square on this sample, as each row is slightly shallower than the width of each square. For this reason it is important to draw your grid as carefully as possible so that you obtain an accurate picture of the finished motif, and to avoid drawing it out of proportion.

4 Now mark your design onto the grid using X to represent each block. Leave the spaces blank so that the motif stands out clearly against the grid.

5 You can use graph paper as an alternative to making your own grid, but you must remember that the proportions differ and the design will appear shallower when the pattern is worked. Calculate the actual size of the motif from the gauge square. For example if you have worked 4 spaces and 5 rows to 2in (5cm) in your sample and your motif takes 12 spaces and 10 rows to complete, you will know that it will measure approximately 6in (15cm) wide × 4in (10cm) deep, and you should plan your design accordingly.

John Hutchinson

Summer chic

White cotton crochet makes a cool, crisp look for summer.
The filet panel features tulip and butterfly motifs.

Sizes
To fit 32[34:36]in (83[87:92]cm) bust.
Length, 18in (46cm).

Note Directions for larger sizes are in
brackets [ ]; if there is only one set of
figures it applies to all sizes.

Materials
*10 x 150yd (137m) or 8oz (200g) of
a lightweight mercerized crochet
cotton
No. 0 (2.00mm) crochet hook*

Gauge
32 sts and 14 rows to 4in (10cm)
measured over crossed doubles on No. 0
(2.00mm) hook.

Note 1 block consists of 3 doubles with 2
doubles for each additional block worked.

Back

Using No. 0 (2.00mm) hook make 138[146:154] ch.

Base row 1dc into 4th ch from hook, 1dc into each ch to end. Turn. 136[144:152] sts.

Beg patt.

1st row 3ch, skip first 2dc, 1dc into next dc, keeping hook at front of work, work 1dc into dc just skipped—called cross 2dc front or Cr2F, (Cr2F) to end, finishing with 1dc into top of 3ch. Turn.

2nd row 3ch, skip first dc, 1dc into next dc, (Cr2F) to last dc and turning ch, 1dc into last dc, 1dc into top of the 3ch. Turn.

These 2 rows form the patt. Cont in patt until work measures 18in (46cm) from beg. Fasten off.

Front side panels (make 2)

Using No. 0 (2mm) hook make 40[44:48] ch. Work base row as for back. 38[42:46] sts. Cont in patt until work measures same as back. Fasten off.

Center front filet panel

Using No. 0 (2.00mm) hook make 63ch. Work base row as for back. 61 sts.

Beg filet pattern.

Next row 4ch, skip first 2dc, *1dc into next dc, 1ch, skip next dc, rep from * to end, finishing with 1dc into top of 3ch. Turn. 30sp. Beg working from chart reading uneven numbered rows (RS) from right to left and even numbered rows (WS) from left to right, until panel measures same as back, working same number of rows. Fasten off.

Join front panels

With WS of center panel facing WS of left front panel and matching foundation chains on each piece rejoin yarn to lower edge and crochet the two pieces tog through double thickness as foll:

Next row 1 ch, 1 sc into same row end as join, *1sc into next row end, 2sc into next row end, rep from * to end, working last sc through edge of both pieces. Turn.

Picot row 1ch, *1sc into each of next 3sc, 3ch, sl st into top of last sc worked—picot formed, rep from * to end, finishing with 1sc into turning ch. Fasten off.

Join right front panel to center panel in same way.

Join shoulder seams on the WS working 1sc into each st along the top edge to the center panel.

Cap sleeves

Mark 22nd[24th:26th] row from shoulder seams on back and front. With RS of work facing join yarn to marked row with sl st, work 2sc into same row end as join, *1sc into next row end, 2sc into next row end, rep from * around armhole to marker. Turn. 66[72:78] sc.

Next row 3ch, skip first 2sc, (Cr2F) to end, finishing with 1dc into last sc. Turn.

Beg row 2 of back, patt 5 rows.

Next row 1 ch, 1 sc into each st to end. Turn.

Picot row 1 ch, *1sc into each of next 3sc, 3ch, sl st into top of last sc worked—picot formed, rep from * to end, finishing 1sc into turning ch. Fasten off.

To finish

Join side seams on WS with sc.

Neck edging

With RS of work facing join yarn to center of back neck and work 1 sc into each st around neck edge, sl st into first sc, do not turn but work a row of picots as before, sl st into first sc. Fasten off.

Lower edging

With RS of work facing join yarn to one side seam and work *1sc into each of next 3sc, skip next ch, rep from * around lower edge, sl st into first sc, do not turn but work a row of picots as before, sl st into first sc. Fasten off.

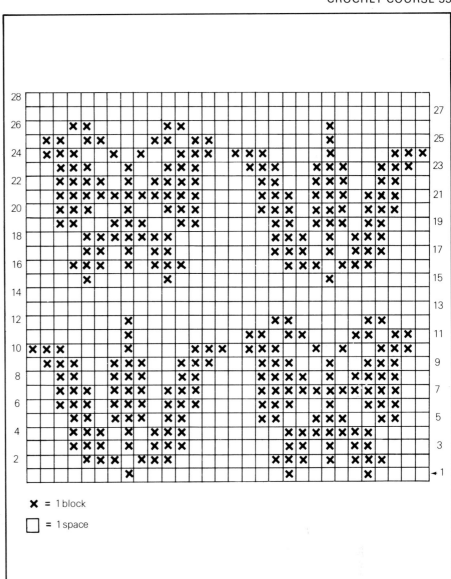

✗ = 1 block

☐ = 1 space

John Hutchinson

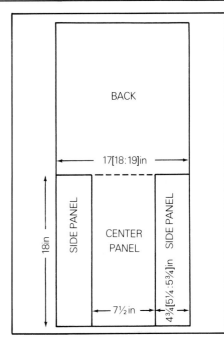

*Narrow vertical and diagonal stripes
*Wide vertical and diagonal stripes
*Working a button loop
*Patterns for girls' sleeveless sweaters

Narrow vertical and diagonal stripes

We have already shown you one method of working narrow vertical stripes (see Knitting course 11, Volume 3, page 26). That method involves using both hands to control the two colors. Here is another way of working vertical stripes in two colors, which can be adapted to produce diagonal stripes. In this method, like the first one, the colors not in use are carried across the back of the work; but both yarns are controlled by the right hand. It is used for stripes five stitches wide, or less. If the stripes are more than five stitches wide, the strands of yarn are likely to be pulled too tightly across the work.

1 To make a two-color striped stockinette stitch fabric with three stitches in the main color (A) and two in the contrasting yarn (B), first cast on the necessary number of stitches with the main color. Use B to knit the first two stitches.

2 Leave color B at the back of the work; pick up A and bring it loosely across from the right-hand row end (over the top of B) to knit the next three stitches. Leave A at the back of the work, pick up B and take it under A to knit the following two stitches. Continue in this way to the end of the row.

3 At the beginning of every row you must have both strands of yarn at the right-hand row end. In this case, color B is already in position, but you must move A to the right over the top of B. Purl the first two stitches with B, catching in A with the first stitch.

4 After purling the first two stitches, leave B at the front of the work. Pick up A and take it loosely across from right-hand row end (over the top of B) to purl next three stitches. Leave A at the front of the work, but over the top of right-hand needle, pick up B and take it under A to purl following two stitches. Continue in this way to end of row.

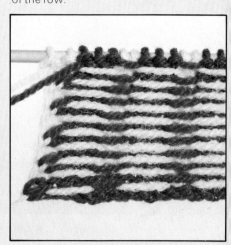

5 Remember to keep the strands of yarn at the back of the work fairly loose; if you pull them tightly you will distort the knitting. On every row you should carry one color above the other consistently (here it is A); this prevents the yarns from becoming tangled.

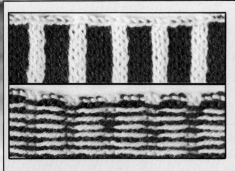

6 The finished fabric looks neat on the right side.
On the wrong side of the work the carried yarns have a regular under-and-over appearance. The carried yarns double the thickness of the fabric.

7 Essentially the same method can be used to make narrow diagonal stripes. The stripes can slope either to the left, as in this picture, or to the right. In this sample the stripes have been moved one stitch to the left on right-side rows and one stitch to the right on wrong-side rows. To do this you change color one stitch *after* you would do so if working vertical stripes on right-side rows and one stitch *before* on wrong-side rows.

8 In this sample the diagonal stripes are sloping to the right. To achieve this gradual slope, you move the stripes one stitch to the right on right-side rows only. You can make an even more gradual slope by working more rows between moving stripes.

Wide vertical and diagonal stripes

If there are more than five stitches in a vertical stripe or if you are using more than two colors, the yarn cannot be carried across the back from one stripe to the next without distorting the tightness of the fabric. Instead, each stripe requires a separate ball of yarn. Unless the stripes are very wide, the separate balls of yarn can be quite small. The most important thing to remember in using individual balls of yarn is to twist each yarn as you start to use it with the one just used, to avoid making a hole in the fabric.

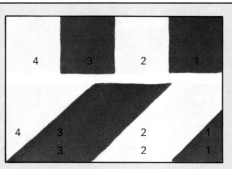

1 Wind small separate balls of yarn, corresponding in number to the maximum number of times you change color across a row. To work the combination of vertical stripes shown at the top, you need four small balls of yarn. The illustration with diagonal stripes requires three balls for the cast-on edge. As new stripes are formed you will need to add new balls at the edge where they begin.

2 To work wide vertical stripes, using the first color, called "A," cast on the required number of stitches for the first stripe; here 10 stitches are needed. Using color B, cast on 10 more stitches. As you work the first stitch of each cast-on group, loop the ball of yarn under and over the color no longer in use.

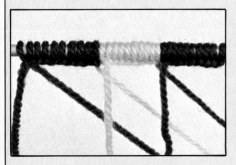

3 Continue in this way until you have cast on the total number of stitches needed; for this sample it is 30. The cast-on edge forms a solid line; instead of each group of stitches being separate, the stripes have been linked together at each color change.

4 To work the first row of a stockinette stitch fabric, use the appropriate ball of yarn to knit to the end of the first stripe. At back of work, pick up second ball of yarn and take it from left to right under and over first color before knitting next stripe. Continue to end.

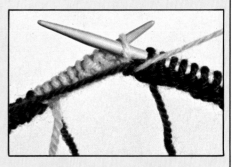

5 On the second (purl) row use the appropriate ball of yarn to purl to the end of the first stripe. Leave the first color slightly to the left at the front (WS). Take second color to the right and over the top of the first color before purling the first stitch in the second stripe.

continued

Fred Mancini

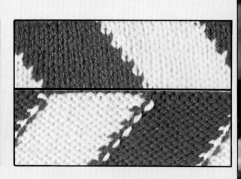

6 Continue in stockinette stitch, always twisting the yarns at each color change; without the twist each stripe would be a separate length of knitting with nothing to link it to the next stripe. The stripe must be joined very neatly, without the twisted colors showing through on the right side. To ensure this, tighten the yarns each time you change color.

7 On the right side of the finished fabric there is no visual sign of a change of yarn except for the color change. The wrong side of the fabric is also neat, with the twisted yarns forming a two-color "rope" at the join.

8 Wide diagonal stripes are worked on the same principle. The diagonal effect is created by gradually moving the stripes to the right or left, one stitch at a time. The desired angle of the slope and the stitch and row gauges of the fabric will determine whether you move a stripe one stitch on every row or only on every two or more rows.

Working a button loop

Button loops are a simple kind of fastening to make, for unlike buttonholes they are not an integral part of the fabric. Instead, they are sewn on the edge of the opening, opposite the button, after the garment is finished. A button loop is ideal for fastening a single button used, for example, at the top of a slash-type neck opening. Only rarely are a number of button loops used to fasten a long row of buttons; in this case, buttonholes are generally preferred.
Obviously, the size of loop varies according to that of the button; generally, the foundation strands of the loop should barely allow the button to pass through, for the loop enlarges when covered with close loop stitches.

1 Thread a blunt-ended yarn needle with yarn matching the garment. Turn the edge of the opening so that it lies horizontally, and join the yarn to the back of the work at the left of the loop position. Insert the needle through edge of fabric the necessary width to the right. Keep loop fairly taut; anchor it at right-hand edge with a small backstitch.

2 Bring the needle back to the first position and make another small stitch, making sure the second strand formed is the same length as the first. Anchor the yarn with a small back stitch. Finally repeat this process at the right-hand end of the loop, so that the foundation has three strands.

3 Turn the work around so that the edge with the loop is facing down. The yarn is now at the left-hand edge of strands. Form it into a large circle below them. Insert the needle from front to back through loop; draw it down and out through the front of the large circle. Tighten the circle over the three strands to form one loop stitch.

4 Continue to work loop stitches over the three strands of yarn until they are completely covered. Although the loop will soon seem to be full of stitches, keep gently pushing them to the left-hand end so that they are as tightly packed as possible.

5 The finished loop overlaps the edge of the opening. It must look neat, with evenly-worked stitches. Pushing the stitches together prevents them from separating later when the loop has become more pliable with use.

Squares and stripes

These trim sweaters are made from simple panels, cleverly arranged to emphasize the diagonal stripes. Worn over turtlenecks, they will keep a teenager warm and cozy when the weather turns chilly.

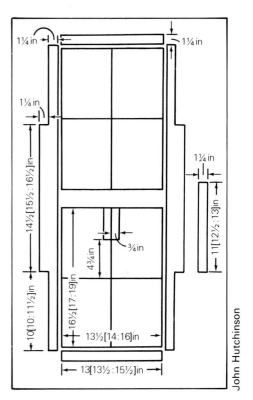

John Hutchinson

Gary Warren

Sizes
To fit chest size 26[28:30]in (66[71:76]cm).
Length, 17¾[18¼:20¼]in (44[46:50]cm).

Note Directions for the larger sizes are in brackets []; where there is only one set of figures it applies to all sizes.

Materials
Narrow-striped top *11[11:13]oz (300[300:350]g) of a knitting worsted in main color (A)*
8[8:9]oz (200[200:250]g) in a contrasting color (B)

Wide-striped top *9[9:11]oz (250[250:300]g) of a knitting worsted in main color (A)*
8[8:9]oz (200[200:250]g) in contrasting color (B)
1 pair No. 8 (5½mm) knitting needles
One button

Gauge
18 sts and 20 rows to 4in (10cm) in narrow-striped patt on No. 8 (5½mm) needles.
16 sts and 20 rows to 4in (10cm) in wide-striped patt on No. 8 (5½mm) needles.

Narrow-striped top
Back
Note Back is worked in four sections.
Lower right-hand section Using No. 8 (5½mm) needles and A, cast on 30[32:36] sts.
1st row (RS) *K2 A, 4 B, rep from * to last 0[2:0] sts, 0[2:0] A.
2nd row PO [1:0] A, 3[4:3] B, *2 A, 4 B, rep from * to last 3 sts, 2 A, 1 B.
3rd row K2 B, *2 A, 4 B, rep from * to last 4[0:4] sts, 2[0:2] A, 2[0:2] B.
4th row P1 [3:1] B, *2 A, 4 B, rep from * to last 5 sts, 2 A, 3 B.
5th row *K4 B, 2 A, rep from * to last 0[2:0] sts, 0[2:0] B.
6th row PO [1:0] B, 1 [2:1] A, *4 B, 2 A, rep from * to last 5 sts, 4 B, 1 A.
These 6 rows form patt. Rep them 5[6:6] times more, then work 5[1:5] rows more. Bind off purlwise with A.
Upper left-hand section Work as for lower right-hand section.
Lower left-hand section Using No. 8 (5½mm) needles and A, cast on 30[32:36] sts.
1st row (RS) KO[2:0] A, *4 B, 2 A, rep from * to end.
2nd row P1 B, 2 A, *4 B, 2 A, rep from * to last 3[5:3] sts, 3[4:3] B, 0[1:0] A.
3rd row K2[0:2] B, 2 [0:2] A, *4 B, 2 A, rep from * to last 2 sts, 2 B.

31

4th row P3 B, 2 A, *4 B, 2 A, rep from * to last 1[3:1] sts, 1[3:1] B.
5th row K0[2:0] B, *2 A, 4 B, rep from * to end of row.
6th row P1 A, 4 B, *2 A, 4 B, rep from * to last 1[3:1] sts, 1[2:1] A, 0[1:0] B.
These 6 rows form patt. Rep them 5[6:6] times more, then work 5[1:5] rows more. Bind off purlwise with A.
Upper right-hand section Work as given for lower left-hand section.

Front

Lower left-hand section Work as given for lower right-hand section of back.
Lower right-hand section Work as given for lower left-hand section of back.
Upper left-hand section Work 24 rows as given for lower left-hand section of back. Work neck edge as follows:
Next row Patt to last 4 sts, K4 A.
Next row K4 A for neck border, patt to end of row.
Complete as given for lower left-hand section of back, working a 4-st border in garter st at neck edge using A.
Upper right-hand section Work 24 rows as given for lower right-hand section of back. Work neck edge:
Next row K4 A, patt to end of row.
Next row Patt to last 4 sts, K4 A.
Complete this section as for lower right-hand section of back, working 4-st border in garter st at neck edge with A.

Lower bands (make 2)

Using No. 8 (5½mm) needles and A, cast on 5 sts. Work 13[13½:15½]in (32[34.5:39]cm) in garter st. Bind off.

Neckband

Using No. 8 (5½mm) needles and A, cast on 5 sts. Work 11[12½:13]in (28[31:33]cm) in garter st. Bind off.

Side bands (make 2)

Using No. 8 (5½mm) needles and A, cast on 5 sts. Work 10[10:11½]in (25[26:29]cm) in garter st.
Next row Cast on 5 sts, K to end. 10 sts.
Cont in garter st until band measures 14½[15½:16½]in (36[38:40]cm) from cast-on sts, ending at same edge as cast-on sts.
Next row Bind off 5 sts, K to end. 5 sts.
Work a further 10[10:11½]in (25[26:29]cm) in garter st. Bind off.

To finish

Pin out each section to correct size. Press or block according to yarn used. Join front and back section using a back stitch seam: take in cast-on and bound-off edges so that they don't show on RS. Join shoulders for 3½[4:4¼]in (9[10:11]cm) from each armhole edge. Sew lower bands in place with flat seam. Sew side bands in position with unshaped edge along side of garment. Sew on neckband, placing each end to

Gary Warren

front opening. Make buttonhole loop at neckband: sew on button. Beg 5½[6:6¼]in (14[15:16]cm) from lower edge, join side seams to end of each armhole. Press seams lightly.

Wide-striped top

Back

Note Back is worked in four sections.
Lower right-hand section Using No. 8 (5½mm) needles cast on 27[30:33] sts as foll: 9[10:11] A, 9[10:11] B, 9[10:11] A.
Next row (WS) P9[10:11] A, 9[10:11] B, 9[10:11] A. Beg patt.
1st row (RS) K9 [10:11] A, 9[10:11] B, 9[10:11] A.
2nd row P8[9:10] A, 9[10:11] B, 9[10:11] A, 1 B.
3rd row K1 B, 9[10:11] A, 9[10:11] B, 8[9:10] A.
4th row P7[8:9] A, 9[10:11] B, 9[10:11] A, 2 B.
5th row K3 B, 9[10:11] A, 9[10:11] B, 6[7:8] A.
6th row P6[7:8] A, 9[10:11] B, 9[10:11] A, 3 B.
Cont in this way, moving diagonals one st to left on K rows and to right on P rows on first, 2nd, 4th and 5th rows of each 6-row patt. Work 7[9:10] rows. This completes corner diagonal.
Cont in this way, moving rem diagonals one st to left on K rows and to right on P rows, until 41[45:50] rows worked

from beg. This completes diagonal.
1st and 3rd sizes only
Rep last row worked once more, using same colors.
All sizes
Using B, bind off.
Lower left-hand section Work as for lower right-hand section, reversing patt by reading row from end to beg and moving diagonal one st to right on K rows and to left on P rows.
Upper right-hand section Using No. 8 (5½mm) needles and B, cast on 27[30:33] sts.
Next row (WS) P1 A, 26[29:32] B. Beg patt.
1st row (RS) K26[29:32] B, 1 A.
2nd row P2 A, 25[28:31] B.
3rd row K25[28:31] B, 2 A.
4th row P3 A, 24[27:30] B.
5th row K23[26:29] B, 4 A.
6th row P4 A, 23[26:29] B.
Work 34[38:43] more rows in this way, moving diagonals one st to right on K rows and to left on P rows on first, 2nd, 4th and 5th rows of each 6-row patt. (A new diagonal must be started at center edge on 29th[31st:35th] row from beg.)
1st and 3rd sizes only
Rep last row worked once more, using same colors.
All sizes
Bind off using colors of last row.
Upper left-hand section Work as for upper right-hand section, reversing patt by reading rows from end to beg and moving diagonal one st to left on K rows and to right on P rows.

Front

Lower left-hand section Work as given for lower right-hand section of back.
Lower right-hand section Work as given for lower left-hand section of back.
Upper left-hand section Patt 24 rows as given for lower left-hand section of back. Work neck edge as foll:
Next row Patt to last 4 sts, K4 A for border.
Next row K 4A for border, patt to end of row.
Complete as given for upper right-hand section of back, working a 4-st border at neck edge using A.
Upper right-hand section Patt 24 rows as given for lower right-hand section of back. Work neck edge:
Next row K4 A, patt to end of row.
Next row Patt to last 4 sts, K4 A.
Complete this section as for upper left-hand section of back, working a 4-st border in garter st at neck edge using A.

Lower, neck and side bands

Work as given for narrow-striped top.

To finish

Complete as for narrow-striped top.

Knitting / COURSE 30

Flat seam

A flat seam in knitting is almost invisible and is ideal for giving a neat, flat finish on stockinette stitch, garter stitch and ribbed sections such as welts. It is used on any straight edge of knitting such as a bound-off shoulder seam—wherever there is no shaping to give a curved or irregular edge to the work.

Use a blunt-ended needle with a large eye for seam knitting: the blunt end will slip between the knitted stitches without splitting the yarn.

Seam knitting with the original yarn whenever possible. Very thick bouclé and some other fancy yarns are sometimes difficult to sew evenly, and in this case it is a good idea to use a 4-ply sport yarn in a matching color.

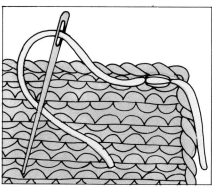

1 Place the right sides of the work together. Match the pattern stitch for stitch and row for row. Join the yarn to the right-hand side of the upper piece.

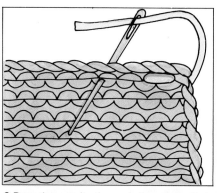

2 Pass the needle through the edge stitch of the lower piece and then back through to the corresponding stitch in the top piece. Pull the yarn through securely.

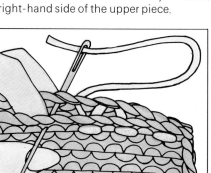

3 Work back through the next stitch on the top piece to the corresponding stitch on the lower piece. Continue working backward and forward in this way until the seam has been completed.

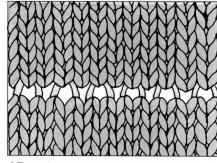

4 Turn the work to the right side and check that the rows have been matched correctly and that the stitches are even. Press the seam carefully so that the inside edge lies flat.

Button fastening at shoulder

Style details such as a button trim at the shoulder give a finishing touch to an otherwise plain garment, and could be incorporated into any straight shoulder seam—for instance, into a variation of the T-shaped sweater. The band for the buttonholes is knitted as part of the front and the band for the buttons forms part of the back. The two bands are overlapped at the shoulder and tacked together while the rest of the garment is made up, and then the buttons are sewn on to close the seam. Contrasting colors or a change of stitch pattern can accentuate the fastening detail. Make sure to overlap the bands so that the buttonholes are uppermost when the work is turned right side out.

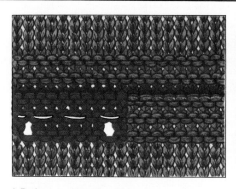

1 Before sewing the right sleeve to the back and front, overlap the buttonhole and button borders on the right shoulder. Pin and tack together so that the knitting stays in place and does not pull out of shape while the sleeve is being sewn in position.

2 Sew the sleeve to the armhole between the markers, sewing through all three thicknesses at shoulder. Remove the tacking thread from the shoulder and sew on the buttons, matching them to the position of the buttonholes.

Please the children and yourself by knitting these dazzling French-style outfits in bouclé yarn.

35

Shorts and sweater

Sizes
Sweater To fit 22[24:26]in (56[61: 66]cm) chest.
Length, 12[13½:15]in (30[34:37]cm).
Sleeve seam, 8¼[10:11½]in (21[25: 29]cm).
Shorts Inner leg seam, 3[3½:4]in (8[9: 10]cm).
Side seam, 9½[10½:11½]in (24[27:29]cm).
Note Directions for larger sizes are in brackets []; if there is only one set of figures it applies to all sizes.

Materials
Sweater: *4[4:5]oz (100[100:120]g) of a medium-weight bouclé or knitting worsted in main color (A) 2oz (40g) in 1st contrasting color (B)*
Shorts: *3[3:4]oz (80[80:100]g) in 1st contrasting color (B) A small ball in main color (A) and 2nd contrasting color (C) 1 pair each Nos. 3 and 4 (3¼ and 3¾mm) knitting needles Three small buttons for sweater Elastic for shorts*

Gauge
24 sts and 36 rows to 4in (10cm) on No. 4 (3¾mm) needles.

Sweater
Front
Using No. 3 (3¼mm) needles and A, cast on 70 [76:82] sts. K11[11:13] rows. Change to No. 4 (3¾mm) needles. Beg with a K row, cont in stockinette st working stripe sequence as foll:
Work 10 rows B, 10 rows A, 8 rows B, 8 rows A, 6 rows B, 6 rows A, 4 rows B, 4 rows A, 2 rows B, 2 rows A, 2 rows B and 2 rows A.
2nd size only Rep last 4 rows twice more.
3rd size only Rep last 4 rows 4 times more. * *
All sizes Work should now measure approx 8[9:10]in (20[23:25]cm). Place a marker at each end of last row to indicate beg of armholes. Working with A only, cont in stockinette st until work measures 3½[4:4½]in (9[10:11]cm) from markers; end with a P row.*** Change to No. 4 (3¾mm) needles.
Next row With A, K48[52:56], join on B, with B K22[24:26].
Next row Join on B, with B K22[24:26], with A K48[52:56].
Buttonhole row With A, K48[52:56], with B, *K2 tog, yo, K6[6:7], rep from * once, K2 tog, yo, K4[6:6].
Next row With B, K22[24:26], with A, K48[52:56].
Next row With A, K48[52:56], with B, K22[24:26].
Keeping colors correct bind off knitwise.

Back
Work as for front to ***. Change to No. 3 (3¼mm) needles. K 4 rows with A.
Next row Join on B, with B, K22[24:26], with A K48[52:56].
Next row With A, bind off 48[52:56], with B, K22[24:26].
K 3 rows with B on rem sts. Bind off knitwise.

Sleeves
Using No. 3 (3¼mm) needles and A, cast on 48[54:60] sts and work as for front to **. Cont in stockinette st with A only, until sleeve measures 8¼[10:11½]in (21[25:29]cm); end with a P row. Bind off loosely.

To finish
Do not press. Using a flat seam, join left shoulder seam. Sew bound off edge of sleeves to armholes between markers, overlapping button and buttonhole bands at shoulder. Join side and sleeve seams. Sew on buttons.

Shorts
Front left leg Using No. 3 (3¼mm) needles and C, cast on 35[39:41] sts. K 5 rows. Change to No. 4 (3¾mm) needles.
1st row (RS) With B, K to end.
2nd row With B, P15[17:18], sl1, P19[21:22].
3rd row With A, K to end.
4th row With A, P15[17:18], sl1, P19[21:22].
5th and 6th rows As 1st and 2nd rows.
7th and 8th rows As 1st and 2nd rows but use C instead of B. Cut off A and B. Cont with C only work as foll:
Next row K19[21:22], K1 winding yarn twice around needle, K15[17:18].
Next row P15[17:18], sl1 dropping extra loop, P19[21:22].
Next row K19[21:22], sl1, K15[17:18].
Next row P15[17:18], sl1 dropping extra loop, P19[21:22].
Cont in this way, keeping slip sts correct, inc one st at end of next row and every foll 4th[6th:6th] row until there are 38[42:44] sts. Work 3[3:7] rows without shaping. Cut off yarn and leave sts on an extra needle.
Right leg Work as for left leg reversing shaping and position of sl st, thus working from the end to the beg of the row as for left leg as foll:
Next row K19[21:22], K1 winding yarn twice around needle, K18[20:21], cast on 2 sts, then work across the sts of left leg thus: K18[20:21], K1 winding yarn twice around needle, K19[21:22]. 78[86:90] sts.
Next row P19[21:22], sl1 dropping extra loop, P38[42:44], sl1 dropping extra loop, P19[21:22].
Next row K19[21:22], sl1, K38[42:44], sl1, K19[21:22].
Next row P19[21:22], sl1, P38[42:44], sl1, P19[21:22].
Work 12 more rows in this way keeping slip sts correct.

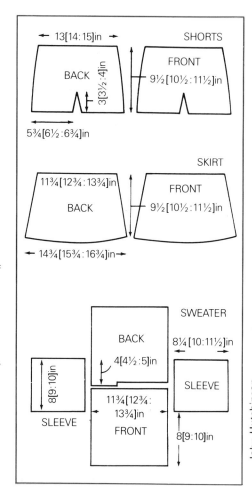

Next row *K16[18:19], sl1, K1, psso, K1, then K1 winding yarn twice around needle, K1, K2 tog, K16[18:19], rep from * to end. 74[82:86] sts.
Next row P18[20:21], sl1 dropping extra loop, P36[40:42], sl1 dropping extra loop, P18[20:21].
Work 14[14:18] more rows keeping slip sts correct.
Next row *K15[17:18], sl1, K1, psso, K1, then K1 winding yarn twice around needle, K1, K2 tog, K15[17:18], rep from * to end. 70[78:82] sts.
Next row P17[19:20], sl1 dropping extra loop, P34[38:40], sl1 dropping extra loop, P17[19:20].
Work 14[18:18] more rows keeping slip sts correct.
Change to No. 3 (3¼mm) needles.
1st ribbing row K1, (P1, K1) to end.
2nd ribbing row P1, (K1, P1) to end.
Rep these 2 rows 3 times more. Bind off loosely in ribbing.

Back
Work as for front.

To finish
Do not press. Join seams. Work herringbone casing over elastic.

Skirt and sweater

Sizes
Sweater To fit 22[24:26]in (56[61: 66]cm) chest.
Length, 12[13½:15]in (30[34:37]cm).
Sleeve seam, 8¼[10:11½]in (21[25:29] cm).
Skirt Length, 9½[10½:11½]in (24[27: 29]cm).
Note Directions for larger sizes are in brackets []; if there is only one set of figures it applies to all sizes.

Materials
Sweater: *4[4:5]oz (100[100:120]g) of a medium-weight bouclé or knitting worsted in main color (A) 2oz (40g) in contrasting color (B)*
Skirt: *3[3:4]oz (80[80:100]g) in main color (A)*
1 pair each Nos. 3 and 4 (3¼ and 3¾mm) knitting needles
Three small buttons for sweater
Elastic for skirt

Gauge
24 sts and 36 rows to 4in (10cm) on No. 4 (3¾mm) needles.

Sweater
Back and front
Work as for sweater back and front of previous outfit.

Sleeves
Using No. 3 (3¼mm) needles and A, cast on 48[54:60] sts. K 5 rows.

Change to No. 4 (3¾mm) needles. Beg with a K row, cont in stockinette st working 2 rows B, 2 rows A and 2 rows B. Cut off B. Cont with A only until sleeve measures 8¼[10:11½]in (21[25:29]cm); end with a P row. Cast off loosely.

To finish
Do not press. Using a flat seam, join left shoulder seam. Sew bound off edge of sleeves to armholes between markers, overlapping button and buttonhole bands at shoulder. Join side and sleeve seams. Sew on buttons.

Skirt
Back and front (alike)
Using No. 4 (3¾mm) needles and A, cast on 178[190:202] sts.
Next row (K2 tog) to end. 89[95:101] sts.
Cont in stockinette st as foll:
1st row (RS) *K29[31:33], K1 winding yarn twice around needle, rep from * once more, K29[31:33].
2nd row *P29[31:33], sl1 dropping extra loop, rep from * once more, P29[31:33].
3rd row *K29[31:33], sl1, rep from * once more, K29[31:33].
4th row As 2nd row.
Rep these 4 rows 4[4:5] times more.
1st dec row *K1, sl 1, K1, psso, K23[25:27], K2 tog, K1, then K1 winding yarn twice around needle, rep from * once more, K1, sl1, K1, psso, K23[25:27], K2 tog, K1. 83[89:95] sts.
Next row *P27[29:31], sl1 dropping extra loop, rep from * once more, P27[29:31].
Work 18[18:22] more rows slipping sts as before.
2nd dec row *K1, sl1, K1, psso, K21[23:25], K2 tog, K1, then K1 winding yarn twice around needle, rep from * once more, K1, sl1, K1, psso, K21[23:25], K2 tog, K1. 77[83:89] sts.
Next row *P25[27:29], sl1, dropping extra loop, rep from * once more, P25[27:29].
Work 18[18:22] more rows slipping sts as before.
3rd dec row *K1, sl1, K1, psso, K19[21:23], K2 tog, K1, then K1 winding yarn twice around needle, rep from * once more, K1, sl1, K1, psso, K19[21:23], K2 tog, K1. 71[77:83] sts.
Next row *P23[25:27], sl1 dropping extra loop, rep from * once more, P23[25:27].
Work 10[18:18] rows without shaping.
Change to No. 3 (3¼mm) needles.
1st ribbing row K1, (P1, K1) to end.
2nd ribbing row P1, (K1, P1) to end.
Rep these 2 rows 3 times more. Bind off loosely in ribbing.

To finish
Do not press. Join side seams. Work herringbone casing over elastic on wrong side of waist ribbing.

Shoestring

Beribboned

Make a pretty tablecloth quickly and easily with a plain piece of fabric and pastel ribbons.

Geoffrey Frosh .

Finished size 42½in (108cm) square.

Materials

1¼yd (1.1m) of 44in (112cm)-wide cotton voile with a woven-in grid pattern

5yd (4.5m) of ⅝in (1.5cm)-wide satin ribbon in each of four different colors

Matching sewing thread

1 Cut voile to 43¼in (110cm) square.

2 Cut each piece of ribbon into four equal lengths.

3 Lay the pieces of ribbon, one of each color, side by side along each side of the fabric square, beginning about 5½in (14cm) in from the edge and working inward.

4 Where the ribbons meet at each corner, weave them in and out of each other.

5 Pin and baste all the ribbons in place.

6 Set your sewing machine to open zig-zag stitch, width ⅛in (2.5mm), length about ⅛in (3mm). Carefully stitch over the edges of the ribbons, working only one line of stitching over the adjoining edges of the ribbon. Cut off excess ribbon in line with edge of fabric.

7 Turn ¼in (5mm) to the wrong side all around the outer edge.

8 Turn under a further ¼in (5mm). Pin and baste hem all around tablecloth neatly, mitering each corner.

9 Topstitch around hem. Finish off ends of threads.

Knitting / COURSE 31

*Slip stitch pattern incorporating weaving
*Slip stitch pattern incorporating drop-stitch technique
*Techniques for working surface-chevron pattern
*Stitch Wise: more slip stitch patterns
*Pattern for a baby's buggy blanket

Slip stitch pattern incorporating weaving

Slip stitch techniques can be used to produce a fabric that is partly knitted and partly woven. In this simple method, one color of yarn is woven into the fabric while the other color is being knitted. The yarn for weaving is never knitted; instead it is threaded in and out of the stitches to form a double strand over two rows.

You must always change colors at the right-hand edge of the knitting and you must always pick up the new color from behind the old one to keep the edge neat. This technique offers tremendous scope for experimenting and, depending on the yarn, can make anything from thick, blanket-like fabrics to glamorous, shimmering ones for evening.

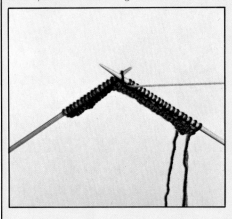

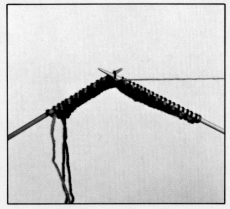

1 Using A, cast on an odd number of stitches. Work the first row (RS): K to end, and 2nd row: K1, P to last st, K1. Use B to work the 3rd row: Sl 1 with yarn in back, *sl 1 with yarn in front, sl 1 with yarn in back, rep from * to end.

2 Use B to work the 4th row: P1, *sl 1 with yarn in back, sl 1 with yarn in front, rep from * to end. Note that B is simply used for weaving in and out of stitches, never for knitting them. It is anchored by the purl stitch at the beginning of this row.

3 Return to A and repeat first and 2nd rows. Use B to work the 7th row: Sl 1 with yarn in front, *sl 1 with yarn in back, sl 1 with yarn in front, rep from * to end and 8th row P1, *sl 1 with yarn in front, sl 1 with yarn in back, rep from * to end. Repeat these 8 rows for the length required.

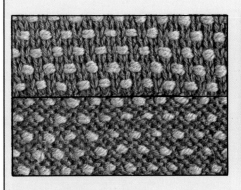

4 This picture shows the finished fabric on both right (top) and wrong sides. It looks equally good on the purl, or wrong, side of the knitting and could easily be reversible.

5 By varying the type of yarn, you can achieve an almost endless range of effects with this weaving technique. Try weaving a metallic yarn against a mohair background, for example.

6 Another variation is to introduce a third color on the 7th and 8th rows as in this colorful, thick fabric worked in bulky yarn.

Fred Mancini

Slip stitch pattern incorporating drop-stitch technique

An interesting texture and color effect can be achieved by combining slip stitch and drop-stitch pattern techniques. Again, the finished fabric looks impressively difficult, yet it is very easy to work.

Dropped stitches are not as dangerous as they sound; they are similar to a cable pattern in that you move them from one position in a row to another, but without the aid of a cable needle. The loop of the stitch is simply left on the surface of the fabric.

The dropped stitches in our sample are all ones that have been slipped during the previous two rows; when you pick them up and work them they make a long stitch, as they stretch from the last row where they were knitted.

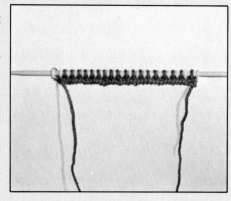

1 Using A, cast on a multiple of 4 stitches plus 2 extra and work the first row: P to end. Use B to work the 2nd row: *K1, sl 1 with yarn in back, rep from * to last 2 sts, K2.

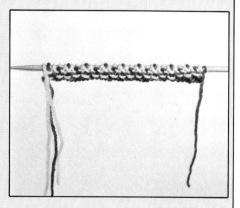

2 With the wrong side of the work facing, again use B to work the 3rd row: P4, *sl 1 with yarn in front, P3, rep from * to last 2 sts, sl 1, P1. The slipped stitches are in A; they were also slipped on the previous row.

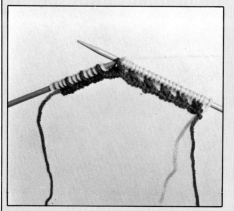

3 The next row contains the drop-stitch technique. Continue using B and work 4th row: *K1, drop slip stitch (in A) off needle and leave at front of work, K2, use left-hand needle to pick up dropped st and K it, rep from * to last 2 sts, K2.

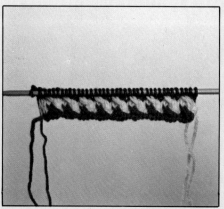

4 Complete the band of color B in the 5th row: P to end. Now use color A to repeat the 2nd, 3rd and 4th rows; that makes 8 pattern rows in all. Repeat these 8 rows for the depth required.

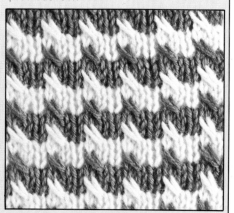

5 The finished fabric has a broken stripe effect. The dropped stitches form long stitches on the surface of the knitting; they are eventually knitted into a different-colored band, so breaking the symmetry of the stripes.

Stitch Wise

Ribbed-tweed pattern

This design uses two colors, A and B, and seed stitch to produce tweed texture and coloring. The "ribs" are vertical lines of slipped stitches in a single color.

Using A, cast on a multiple of 4 sts plus 3 extra.

1st row (RS) Using A, P1, *K1, P1, rep from * to end.

2nd row Using A, as first.

3rd row Using B, P1, K1, P1, *sl 1 with yarn in back, P1, K1, P1, rep from * to end.

4th row Using B, P1, K1, P1, *sl 1 with yarn in front, P1, K1, P1, rep from * to end.

Rep these 4 rows throughout.

This pattern also works very well in a mixture of mohair and knitting worsted yarn. Using the mohair as color A, the slip stitch "ribs" are in mohair bordering a softly mixed section of tweed in both yarns. When the yarns are alternated and the knitting worsted is color A, the tweed stitches have much harsher outlines.

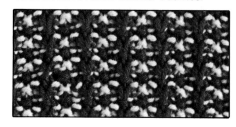

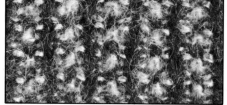

Techniques for working surface-chevron pattern

Surface-chevron pattern (see Stitch Wise, below) incorporates all the best aspects of slip stitch patterns to form a thick, intricate-looking fabric suitable for outdoor wear.

The pattern consists of horizontal bands of two alternating colors with long, dropped stitches in one color forming interlocking V shapes and stretching across the next band in the other color. The main pattern row (6) is not as complicated as it looks. The step-by-step sequence given here will help you master the dropped-stitch technique required for this pattern.

The dropped stitches have extra interest because they are long stitches made by winding the yarn an extra number of times around the needle before working a stitch.

1 On the first and 5th rows you must prepare the long stitches. Bring the yarn to the front after knitting the last stitch in a group, then wind it completely around the right-hand needle *twice* before purling the next stitch.

2 On the next row you must drop the extra loops made by winding the yarn twice around the needle in order to form long stitches. Simply remove the left-hand needle from the two extra stitches: a long loop results.

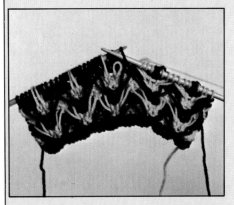

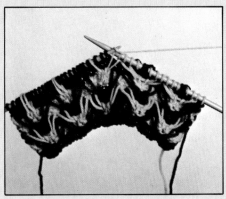

3 Transfer position of previous long, slip stitches: move the first to the right and the second to the left. Drop next long stitch—don't worry, it won't unravel. Slip last three stitches on right-hand needle back onto left-hand needle.

4 Use right-hand needle to pick up dropped stitch and replace it on left-hand needle. Knit the long, dropped stitch, making sure that it isn't twisted. The pattern directions tell you how to move the other long stitch.

5 At the end of the main pattern row pairs of long stitches have been moved to the right and left to form a V shape. The new long stitches are in the center of the V. The V stitches give a chevron appearance to the finished fabric.

Fred Mancini

Stitch Wise

Surface-chevron pattern

You require two colors, A and B. Using A, cast on a multiple of 8 sts plus 2 extra. (See techniques for working pattern, above.)

1st row (WS) Using A, K4, * (yarn twice over needle—called yo twice, P1) twice, K6, rep from * ending with K4 instead of K6.

2nd row Using B, K4, *with yarn in back sl 2 dropped extra loops, K6, rep from * ending with K4.

3rd row Using B, K4, *with yarn in front sl 2, K6, rep from * ending with K4.

4th row As 3rd, slipping sts with yarn in back.

5th row Using B, K3, *yo twice, P1, with yarn in front sl 2, yo twice, P1, K4, rep

from * ending with K3.

6th row Using A, K1, *sl 3 dropping loops from 3rd st, drop first long st off needle at front, sl same 3 sts back onto left-hand needle, pick up and K dropped st, K2, sl 1 with yarn in back, drop 2nd long st off needle at front, sl 3 dropping loops from first st, pick up dropped st on left-hand needle, sl 3rd and 2nd of last slipped sts back onto left-hand needle, K3, rep from * ending with K1.

7th-10th rows As 3rd-6th, reversing colors.

Rep the 3rd-10th rows inclusive throughout.

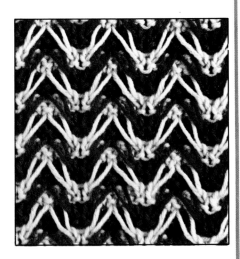

Cozy cover-up

Make this red, white and blue buggy blanket in a bulky yarn for extra warmth.

Size
24¾in (63cm) long by 20¾in (52cm) wide.

Materials
8oz (200g) of a bulky-weight yarn in main color (A)
4oz (100g) each of contrasting colors (B and C)
1 pair each of Nos. 8 and 10 (5½ and 6½mm) needles

Gauge
14 sts to 4in (10cm) in patt on No. 10 (6½mm) needles.

Center panel
Using No. 10 (6½mm) needles and A, cast on 62 sts. K1 row. Beg patt.
1st row (RS) Using B, K1, sl 1, *K4, sl 2, rep from * to last 6 sts, K4, sl 1, K1.
2nd row Using B, P1, sl 1, *P4, sl 2, rep from * to last 6 sts, P4, sl 1, P1.
3rd row Using A, as first.
4th row Using A, K1, with yarn in front sl 1, take yarn to back, *K4, sl 2 with yarn in front, take yarn to back, rep from * to last 6 sts, K4, sl 1 with yarn in front, take yarn to back, K1.
5th row Using C, K3, *sl 2, K4, rep from * to last 5 sts, sl 2, K3.
6th row Using C, P3, *sl 2, P4, rep from * to last 5 sts, sl 2, P3.
7th row Using A, as 5th.
8th row Using A, K3, *sl 2 with yarn in front, take yarn to back, K4, rep from * to last 5 sts, sl 2 with yarn in front, take yarn to back, K3.
These 8 rows form patt. Rep until work measures approx 21½in (55cm) from beg; end with 7th row. Bind off in A.

Border
Using No. 8 (5½mm) needles and A, cast on 6 sts. Work 7¾in (20cm) in garter st.
Shape corner
1st row K5, turn.
2nd row Sl 1, K4.
3rd row K4, turn.
4th row Sl 1, K3.
5th row K3, turn.
6th row Sl 1, K2.
7th row K2, turn.
8th row Sl 1, K1.
9th and 10th rows As 7th and 8th.
11th and 12th rows As 5th and 6th.
13th and 14th rows As 3rd and 4th.
15th and 16th rows As first and 2nd.
Cont in garter st for length of one long side, ending at outer edge. Rep 16 corner rows, then cont for length of short edge. Rep corner, then cont for length of long

side. Rep corner, then cont until this piece meets first piece along short edge. Bind off.

To finish
Press or block center panel according to yarn used. Join cast-on and bound-off seam on border and sew in position all around center panel. Press seams.

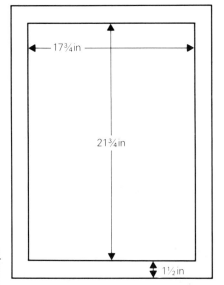

Brian Mayor

17¾in
21¾in
1½in

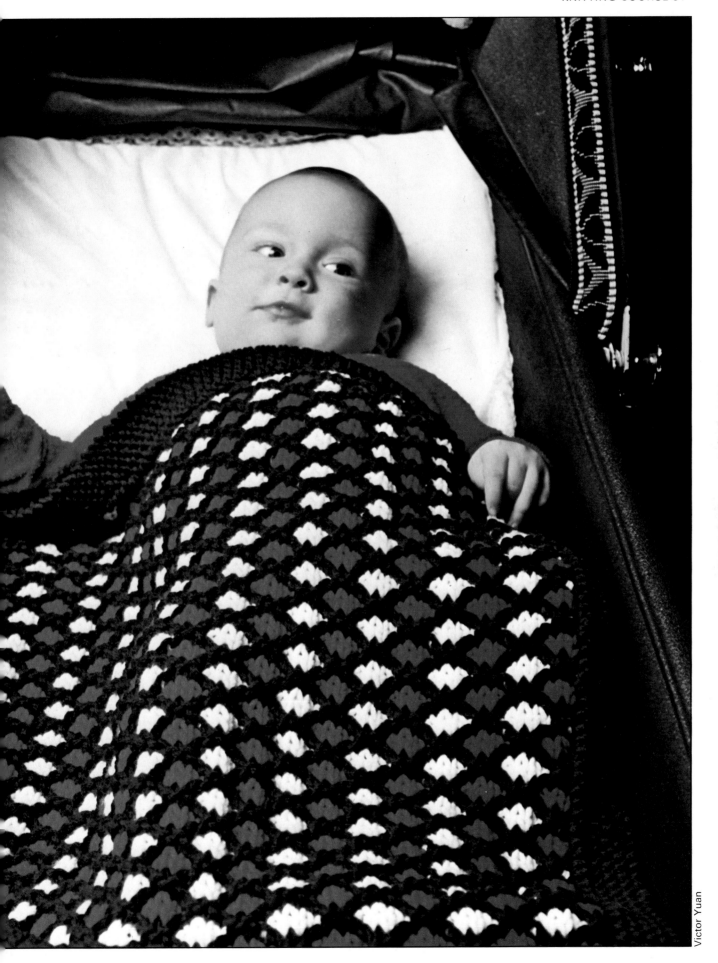

Double casting on

Experiment with this unusual method of casting on—you may find it easier than the one you are already using. The working method appears to be a combination of previous techniques—using your thumb to cast on with two needles. Both needles are held in your right hand throughout and operate as a single needle. A double cast-on is often used by professional knitters wherever a strong, but elastic, edge is needed. It makes an ideal cast-on edge for the ribbed back of the man's vest on page 47.

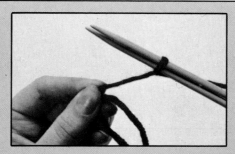

1 Hold the two needles together in your right hand. Make a slip knot some distance from the end of a ball of yarn and put it on the needles. (1yd [1m] of knitting worsted makes about 60 stitches.) The short end is for making the stitches in the same way as casting on with one needle.

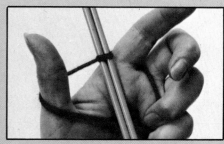

2 Take both ends of yarn—that from the main ball and the short end—and hold them together across the palm of your left hand. The short end is around your thumb and the yarn from the main ball around your index finger.

3 Use both needles together to cast on the stitches: put them up through the loop on the front of the thumb and down through the loop on the index finger, drawing a new stitch through the loop on the thumb.

4 Release the loop on your thumb; without letting go of either end of yarn in your left hand, tighten the new loop on the needles by re-inserting your thumb under the short end and pulling it gently downward.

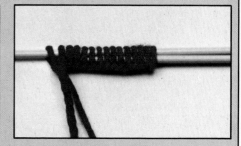

5 Repeat steps 3 and 4 until you have cast on the required number of stitches. Withdraw one of the needles. Transfer the needle with the stitches to your left hand and hold the free needle in your right hand ready to begin knitting.

Mosaic-pattern effects

Mosaic patterns are a sophisticated version of slip stitch design. They use two colors of yarn, which alternate every two rows; the colors are worked with slip-stitch techniques to create unusual geometric shapes. The design appears when part of the pattern in one color is hidden behind slip stitches of a different colored yarn, coming from a row below. The slip stitches span two rows and are caught up again by their own color on the third row. Mosaic designs are very versatile: they can be worked over any number of stitches as there are no special instructions for wrong-side rows.

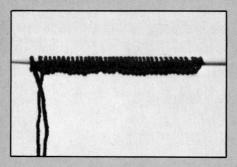

1 You need two colors of yarn, A and B. Color A forms the pattern, while B is the background. Using B, cast on a multiple of 6 stitches plus 2 extra. Knit the first 2 rows.

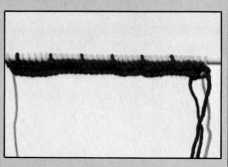

2 Join in A and use it to work the 3rd row (RS) K6, *sl 1, K5, rep from * to last 2 sts, sl 1, K1. Note that on all right-side rows you must keep the yarn in the back when slipping stitches.

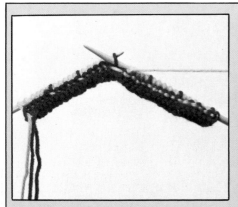

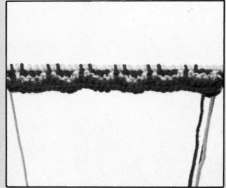

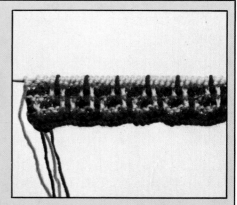

3 On the 4th row and all other wrong-side rows, use the same color as the previous row to knit the same stitches as before; slip the same stitches, remembering to keep the yarn at the front of the work.

4 Use B to work the 5th row K1, sl 1, *K3, sl 1, K1, sl 1, rep from * ending last rep with K2. For the 7th row using A, K4, *sl 1, K1, sl 1, K3, rep from * ending with K1. The pattern is now beginning to form.

5 Use B to work the 9th row K3, *sl 1, K1, sl 1, K3, rep from * ending with K2. For the 11th row, using A, K4, *sl 1, K5, rep from * ending with K3. Work the next wrong-side row to complete 12 pattern rows.

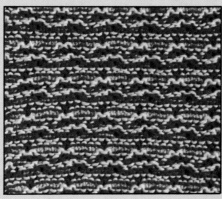

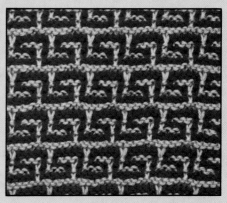

6 Repeat the 12 pattern rows throughout until the fabric is the required depth. Cast off after working the first two rows using B. Color A makes horizontal bands of a formal, "key-type" pattern.

7 The back of a mosaic-patterned fabric is very neat. The fabric is only a single thickness unlike the double thickness of colorwork knitting where two yarns are carried across a row of knitting.

8 You can achieve an interesting, and often completely different, effect if you reverse the colors in the design. Here the previous color A has been used for the background, while B forms the design. Choose two contrasting light and dark colors to give the most pronounced results.

9 Give a greater emphasis to the pattern by having the design in garter stitch against a stockinette stitch background. Simply purl the wrong-side rows worked in B, the background color.

10 Most mosaic patterns are entirely in garter stitch, but there is no rule against working them in stockinette stitch. The finished fabric is not textured and the stitch gauge of the work makes the designs taller and thinner.

11 You can experiment with different types of yarn to achieve varying effects and textures. Top, a mohair pattern has been worked against a knitting worsted background. Below, a shiny crepe yarn is used against a sport yarn background.

Mike Berend

Stitch Wise

Alternating checks

You require two colors, A and B. Using A, cast on a multiple of 14 sts plus 2 extra. Note that on all rows, you must slip stitches with the yarn at the back.

1st and 2nd rows Using A, K to end.
3rd, 7th, 11th and 15th rows (RS) Using B, K1, *K7, (sl 1, K1) 3 times, sl 1, rep from * to last st, K1.
4th and foll alternate rows K all sts knitted in previous row with same color and sl all slipped sts with yarn in front.
5th, 9th and 13th rows Using A, K1, *(sl 1, K1) 3 times, sl 1, K7, rep from * to last st, K1.
17th and 18th rows Using A, K to end.
19th, 23rd, 27th and 31st rows Using B, as 5th.
21st, 25th and 29th rows Using A, as 3rd.
32nd row As 4th.
These 32 rows form the patt. Rep them throughout.

Fancy border pattern

You require two colors, A and B. Using A, cast on a multiple of 16 sts plus 2 extra. Note that on all right-side rows you must slip stitches with the yarn in back.

1st row (RS) Using B, K1, *K4, sl 1, K11, rep from * to last st, K1.
2nd and every foll alternate row P or K (depending on whether you want stockinette st or garter st fabric) all sts knitted in previous row with the same color and sl all slipped sts with yarn in front.
3rd row Using A, K1, *(K3, sl 1) twice, (K1, sl 1) 3 times, K2, rep from * to last st, K1.
5th row Using B, K1, *K2, sl 1, K3, sl 1, K7, sl 1, K1, rep from * to last st, K1.
7th row Using A, K1, *K1, (sl 1, K3) twice, sl 1, K1, sl 1, K3, sl 1, rep from * to last st, K1.
9th row Using B, K1, *K4, (sl 1, K3) 3 times, rep from * to last st, K1.
11th row Using A, K1, *(K3, sl 1) 3 times, K4, rep from * to last st, K1.
13th row Using B, K1, *sl 1, K3, sl 1, K1, (sl 1, K3) twice, sl 1, K1, rep from * to last st, K1.
15th row Using A, K1, *K1, sl 1, K7, sl 1, K3, sl 1, K2, rep from * to last st, K1.
17th row Using B, K1, *K2, (sl 1, K1) 3 times, (sl 1, K3) twice, rep from * to last st, K1.
19th row Using A, K1, *K11, sl 1, K4, rep from * to last st, K1.
20th row As 2nd.
These 20 rows form the patt.

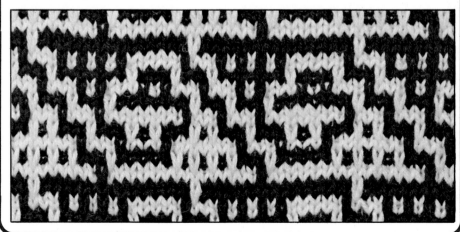

Sporty colors

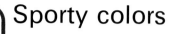

A simple slip stitch pattern gives you sporty color combinations.

Sizes
To fit 36[38:40:42]in (92[97:102:107] cm) chest. Length to shoulder, 21¼[21¾: 22:22½]in (54[55:56:57]cm).

Note Directions for larger sizes are in brackets []; if there is only one set of figures it applies to all sizes.

Materials

7[8:8:9]oz (200[225:225:250]g) of a fingering yarn in main color (A)
2[3:3:3]oz (50[75:75:75]g) in a contrasting color (B)
1 pair each Nos. 2 and 3 (3 and 3¼mm) knitting needles
5 buttons

Gauge

32 sts to 4in (10cm) over main ribbing patt on No. 3 (3¼mm) needles.

Back

Using No. 2 (3mm) needles and A, cast on 143[151:159:167] sts.
1st row K2, *P1, K1, rep from * to last st, K1.
2nd row K1, *P1, K1, rep from * to end.
Rep these 2 rows for ¾in (2cm); end with a 2nd row.
Change to No. 3 (3¼mm) needles. Beg main ribbing patt

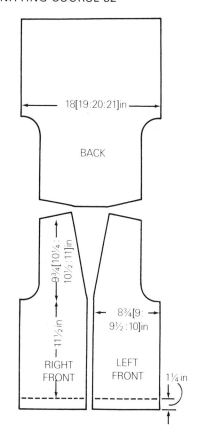

John Hutchinson

18[19:20:21]in

BACK

9¾[10¼: 10½:11]in

11½in

8¾[9: 9½:10]in

RIGHT FRONT

LEFT FRONT

1¼ in

1st row (RS) K to end.
2nd row K1, *P1, K1, rep from * to end.
These 2 rows form patt. Cont in patt until work measures 11½in (29cm) from beg; end with 2nd row.

Shape armholes
Bind off 7[9:10:11] sts at beg of next 2 rows. Dec one st at each end of next 5[5:7:7] rows, then at each end of every other foll row until 103[107:111:115] sts rem. Cont straight until work measures 21¼[21¾:22:22½]in (54[55:56:57]cm) from beg; end with 2nd row.

Shape shoulders
Bind off 11[11:12:12] sts at beg of next 4 rows and 10[11:11:12] sts at beg of next 2 rows. Bind off.

Right front
Using No. 2 (3mm) needles and A, cast on 69[73:77:81] sts. Beg with K row, work 9 rows stockinette st.
Next row K to end to mark foldline. Change to No. 3 (3¼mm) needles. Beg patt.
1st row (RS) Using A, K to end.
2nd row Using A, P to end.
3rd row Using B, K4, *sl 1, K3, rep from * to last st, K1.
4th row Using B, K4, *sl 1 with yarn in front, take yarn to back, K3, rep from * to last st, K1.
5th row Using A, K1, *sl 1, K1, rep from * to end.
6th row Using A, P1, *sl 1, P1, rep from * to end.
7th row Using B, K2, *sl 1, K3, rep from * ending with K2.

8th row Using B, K2, *sl 1 with yarn in front, take yarn to back, K3, rep from * ending with K2.
9th and 10th rows Using A, as first and 2nd.
11th and 12th rows Using B, as 7th and 8th.
13th and 14th rows Using A, as 5th and 6th.
15th and 16th rows (B), as 3rd and 4th. These 16 rows form patt. Cont in patt until work measures 11½in (29cm) from hemline; end with WS row.

Shape armhole and front edge
Next row K2 tog, patt to end.
Next row Bind off 8[10:11:12] sts, patt to end.
Dec one st at armhole edge on next 5[5:7:7] rows, then on foll 8[8:7:8] alternate rows. *At same time* dec one st at front edge on 3rd and every foll 4th row until 34[36:39:39] sts rem, then on every foll 6th row until 30[31:33:34] sts rem. Cont straight until work measures same as back to shoulder excluding hem; end at armhole edge.

Shape shoulders
Bind off 10[10:11:11] sts at beg of next and foll alternate row. Work 1 row. Bind off.

Left front
Work as for right front, reversing shaping.

Armhole borders
Join shoulder seams. Using No. 2 (3mm) needles, A and with RS of work facing, pick up and K 181[187:195:199] sts around armhole. Beg with a 2nd row, rib 7 rows as for back lower edge. Bind off in ribbing.

Front band
Mark button positions on right front edge with pins, with top one just below beg of front edge shaping and last one ½in (1cm) above foldline, and 3 more evenly spaced between. Using No. 2 (3mm) needles and A, cast on 11 sts. Work in ribbing as for back lower edge until band, slightly stretched, fits up left front edge, across back neck and down right front edge. Make buttonholes to match markers as foll:
1st buttonhole row Rib 4, bind off 3, rib to end.
2nd buttonhole row Rib to end, casting on 3 sts over those bound off in last row.

To finish
Turn hem to WS at foldline and slip stitch in place. Join side and armhole border seams.
Sew front band in place.
Sew on buttons to correspond with buttonholes.

Knitting / COURSE 33

Working a square neckline with a ribbed neckband

Square necklines are easy to work as they need a minimum of shaping. Basically you work to the position of the front (or back) neckline, leave a number of front neck stitches on a holder and complete each side of the neck separately without shaping it. The neckline is later finished with a band. The ribbed neckband shown here is slightly different—and even easier to work—as the center front ribbed band is worked in one with the main fabric. After the neckline is complete you need only pick up stitches down the sides of the neck. This neckband requires no shaping: you can use a set of four needles to work in rows if you want to avoid a seam at one shoulder.

1 Work to point of lower edge of neckline, ending with a wrong-side row. Continue across all stitches, working the center (neck) stitches in ribbing. Here you need a multiple of 4+2 stitches to work in K2, P2 ribbing, beginning and ending right-side rows with P2.

2 Continue in this way until the ribbing is required depth—usually ½in to 1in (1.5 to 2.5cm), ending with a wrong-side row. On the next row, work until you reach the ribbing, then slip the remaining stitches on the left-hand needle onto a holder.

3 Turn work and complete left side of the neck first. Work in pattern—slipping the first stitch at neck edge on alternate rows—for the required depth: there is no need for shaping at either neck or armhole edge. Follow pattern for shaping shoulder.

4 Return to stitches on holder: replace them on a needle. With right side of work facing, rejoin yarn to ribbing stitches and bind them off in ribbing. Work to end of row.

5 The remaining stitches are for the second (right) side of the neck; they must correspond in number to those in the left side. Complete the right side of the neck to match the left.

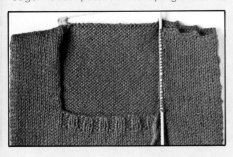

6 Join the right shoulder seam on front and back sections. Turn the work right side out. Using two sizes smaller needles, pick up and knit an even number of stitches down left side of neck.

7 Change to needles used for fabric. Work the same number of ribbing rows as in the center front neckband. Bind off loosely in ribbing.

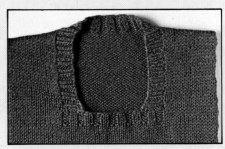

8 Complete other side of neck—including back neck stitches—to match. Join left shoulder and neckband seams. At front neck join ends of neckband to bound-off stitches.

Fred Mancini

49

Working a garter stitch neckband with mitered corners

Instead of a ribbed neckband, it is often prettier, especially with a square neckline, to use garter stitch. In this case the entire neckband is picked up and worked after the front and back sections are complete.

The right-angled corners of this neckline must be mitered to continue the square shape and allow the neckband to lie flat. Mitering consists of decreasing at each side of a central line (here it is a stitch) passing at a 45-degree angle through the corner.

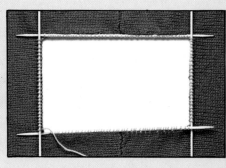

1 When the front and back sections are complete, join the shoulder seams in the usual way. Here the back also has a square neckline—as does the dress in the pattern on page 51: the front and back neck stitches are on holders.

2 With the right side of the work facing and using a set of four needles two sizes smaller than those used for the main fabric (you can also use a circular needle if there are enough stitches), begin at one shoulder and pick up and knit stitches all around neck as instructed in pattern.

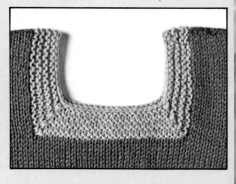

3 To establish four corner stitches at front and back necks, purl (for alternate rows of garter stitch in rounds) until one stitch remains on the first side you picked up along: purl this stitch together with the first stitch of the next side. Continue in this way, decreasing four times in all, until the round is complete.

4 Knit alternate rounds without shaping. On following purl rounds you must always purl three stitches together at each corner. The decrease group consists of the single stitch remaining from previous decrease coupled with one stitch from each side of it.

5 Each time you purl three stitches together, the original number of stitches you picked up along a side of the neckline reduces by two. Bind off on a purl round, working the four decreases as before.

Techniques for working a flared edge

A flared edge makes an attractive and unusual finish for a dress, coat or skirt hemline: it works especially well when the skirt section of the garment is knitted downward in an alternating narrow and wide ribbing pattern. This enables you to continue knitting directly into the "flares" which form over any number of rows (to give the required depth of hemline) by increasing the original narrow ribbing stitches into a triangular shape. The original number of wide ribbing stitches between flares remains constant. When the edge is bound off the triangular flares curve into a fluted edge.

Row-by-row directions for this edge are given in the dress pattern on page 51, follow the guidelines shown here for help in working it or adapting the technique for other fabrics.

1 At the lower edge of the skirt you have wide reverse stockinette stitch ribbing sections separated by narrow, single "knit" ribs. To begin shaping the flares, you must increase on each side of the ribs by picking up the horizontal strand of yarn between stitches and knitting it through the back of the loop.

2 Follow the same formula for working the next and every other wrong-side row —knit the stitches in the sections between flares and purl those in the flares. The number of stitches in the flares increases with each right-side row: here it is three.

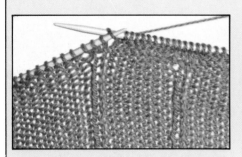 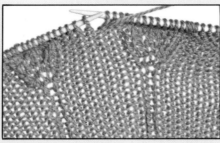 

3 On the third shaping row increase each side of the center flare stitch to make five stitches out of three. Thereafter, on the next and every following right-side row, the formula for increasing two stitches in each flare is the same—increase one stitch two stitches from each end.

4 Continue to increase one stitch within a two-stitch border at each side of the flare in right-side rows. From a single rib stitch each flare extends into a triangular shape.

5 When the flared edge is the required depth, ending with a right-side row, knit two rows. Bind off loosely knitwise. When the stitches are free of the needles the flares curve outward to form a fluted edge.

Fun flares

Flared shaping at the hem creates a flounced, feminine-looking dress. Wear it to work as an overdress, or by itself as a sundress.

Sizes
To fit 32[34:36]in (83[87:92]cm) bust. Length, 41[41¾:42½]in (104[106:108] cm).
Note Directions for larger sizes are in brackets []; if there is only one set of figures it applies to all sizes.

Materials
25[27:29]oz (700[750:800]g) of a knitting worsted-weight novelty yarn
1 pair each Nos. 2 and 4 (3 and 3¾mm) knitting needles
Set of four No. 2 (3mm) double-pointed needles or No. 2 (3mm) circular needle

Gauge
21 sts and 30 rows to 4in (10cm) in stockinette st worked on No. 4 (3¾mm) needles.

Back yoke
Using No. 2 (3mm) needles cast on 88[97:106] sts. Work 6 rows garter st. Change to No. 4 (3¾mm) needles. Beg with K row, cont in stockinette st until work measures 2in (5cm); end with P row.
Next row K to last 13[14:15] sts, turn and leave rem sts on holder.
Next row P to last 13[14:15] sts, turn and leave rem sts on holder.
Cont straight on rem 62[69:76] sts until armholes measure 4[4¼:4¾]in (10[11:12] cm); end with P row.
Divide for neck
K10[12:14] turn and complete right side

of neck. Cont until armhole measures 8[8¾:9½]in (20[22:24]cm); end with P row. Bind off. Return to rem sts, sl first 42[45:48] sts on holder for back neck, rejoin yarn to next st and K to end. Match left side of neck to right.

Front yoke
Work as for back yoke.

Back skirt
Using No. 4 (3¾mm) needles and with RS facing, pick up and K 88[97:106] sts along cast-on edge of yoke.
Next row (WS) K5[6:7], *P1, K10[11:12], rep from * 6 times, P1, K5[6:7].
Next row P5[6:7], *K1, P10[11:12], rep from * 6 times more, K1, P5[6:7].
Rep the last 2 rows 9 times more, then the first of them again.
Next row P5[6:7], *K1, P5[5:6], pick up loop lying between needles and P tbl—called make one purlwise or M1 P-wise, P5[5:6], rep from *6 times more, K1, P to end. 95[104:113] sts.
Next row K5[6:7], *P1, K11[12:13], rep from * 6 times more, P1, K to end. Work 22 rows as set.
Next row P1, M1 P-wise, P4[5:6], *K1, P5[6:6], M1 P-wise, P6[6:7], rep from * 6 times more, K1, P to last st, M1 P-wise, P1. 104[113:122] sts.
Next row K6[7:8], *P1, K12[13:14], rep from * 6 times more, P1, K to end. Work 22 rows as set.
Next row P6[7:8], *K1, P6[6:7], M1 P-wise, P6[7:7], rep from * 6 times more, K1, P to end. 111[120:129] sts.
Next row K6[7:8], *P1, K13[14:15], rep from * 6 times more, P1, K to end. Work 22 rows as set.
Next row P1, M1 P-wise, P5[6:7], *K1, P6[7:7], M1 P-wise, P7[7:8], rep from * 6 times more, K1, P to last st, M1, P1. 120[129:138] sts.
Cont in this way, inc in each panel on every 24th row and at each end on every 48th row, until there are 152[161:170] sts. Cont straight until work measures 37[37¾:38½]in (94[96:98]cm) from shoulder, or 4in (10cm) less than final length; end with WS row.

Shape flared edge
1st row P9[10:11], *pick up loop lying between needles and K tbl—called make one knitwise or M1 K-wise, K1 M1 K-wise, P18[19:20], rep from * 6 times more, M1 K-wise, K1, M1 K-wise, P to end.
2nd row K9[10:11], *P3, K18[19:20], rep from * 6 times more, P3, K to end.
3rd row P9[10:11], *(K1, M1 K-wise) twice, K1, P18[19:20], rep from * 6 times more, (K1, M1 K-wise) twice, K1, P to end.
4th row K9[10:11], *P5, K18[19:20], rep from * 6 times more, P5, K to end.
5th row P9[10:11], *K2, M1 K-wise, K1, M1 K-wise, K2, P18[19:20], rep from * 6 times more, K2, M1 K-wise, K1, M1 K-wise, K2, P to end.

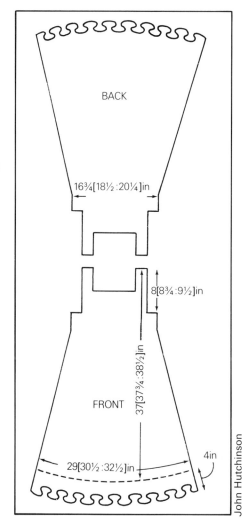

BACK

16¾[18½:20¼]in

8[8¾:9½]in

37[37¾:38½]in

FRONT

29[30½:32½]in

4in

John Hutchinson

Gary Warren

6th and every alternate row K or P sts as necessary.
7th row P9[10:11], *K2, M1 K-wise, K3, M1 K-wise, K2, P18[19:20], rep from * 6 times more, K2, M1 K-wise, K3, M1 K-wise, K2, P to end.
9th row P9[10:11], *K2, M1 K-wise, K5, M1 K-wise, K2, P18[19:20], rep from * 6 times more, K2, M1 K-wise, K5, M1 K-wise, K2, P to end.
11th row P9[10:11], *K2, M1 K-wise, K7, M1 K-wise, K2, P18[19:20], rep from * 6 times more, K2, M1 K-wise, K7, M1 K-wise, K2, P to end.
Cont in this way, working 2 more sts between incs in each section, until there are 25 sts between incs (on 29th row); end with RS row.
Change to No. 2 (3mm) needles. K2 rows. Bind off.

Front skirt
Work as for back skirt.

Neckband
Join shoulders. Using four No. 2 (3mm) needles or circular needle and with RS facing, start at a shoulder seam and pick up and K 21[23:25] sts to corner, K across sts on holder, pick up and K 42[46:50] sts along other side of neck, K across sts on holder, pick up and K 21[23:25] sts to shoulder. 168[182:196] sts.
Next round P20[22:24], P2 tog, P40[43:46], P2 tog, P40[44:48], P2 tog, P40[43:46], P2 tog, P20[22:24].
Next round K to end.
Next round P19[21:23], P3 tog, P38[41:44], P3 tog, P38[42:46], P3 tog, P38[41:44], P3 tog, P19[21:23].
Work 5 more rounds, dec as shown at each corner on P rounds. Bind off purlwise, dec as before.

Armhole borders
With No. 2 (3mm) needles and RS facing, K across 13[14:15] sts left at underarm, pick up and K 84[92:100] sts around armhole, K across other 13[14:15] sts. 110[120:130] sts.
Next row K12[13:14], K3 tog, K to last 15[16:17] sts, K3 tog, K to end.
Next row K to end.
Next row K11[12:13], K3 tog, K to last 14[15:16] sts, K3 tog, K to end.
K 5 more rows, dec on WS rows. Bind off knitwise, dec as before.

To finish
Press or block according to yarn used. Be careful not to flatten ribbing. Join side seams. Press seams.

Sewing / COURSE 28

*Collar bands
*Cutting a collar band from an all-in-one collar
*Pattern for a smocked dress

Collar bands

A collar band is sometimes used by itself—without a collar—to finish the neckline of a dress or blouse. (Used in this way, it is also called a mandarin collar.) You can easily adapt some shirt or blouse patterns for this style—as we have done to make the dress on page 54. If the collar is cut in two parts, you can simply use the collar band and omit the collar itself.

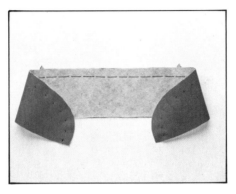

1 Cut out and baste interfacing to the wrong side of one collar band section.

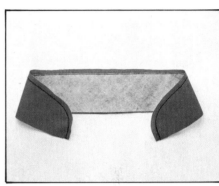

2 Baste and stitch the two collar bands together, leaving the neck edge open. Grade the seam allowances, trimming the interfacing close to the stitching.

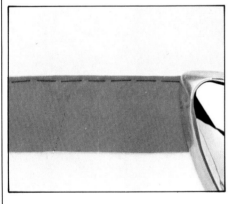

3 Turn the collar band right side out and baste around the stitched edges. Press.

4 Baste and stitch the interfaced edge of the collar band to the neck edge of the garment. Grade the seams, trimming the interfacing close to the stitching, and clip the neck curve at intervals. Press the seam up toward the band.

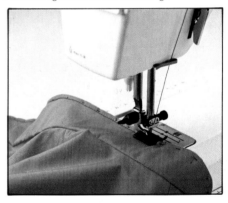

5 Turn in the seam allowance of the inner band and slip stitch it to the stitching line. Press. Add a line of topstitching $\frac{1}{4}$in (6mm) from the outer edge of the band.

Paul Williams

Cutting a collar band from an all-in-one collar

If the collar and band are cut all-in-one in the pattern you are adapting, it is still quite easy to cut a collar band to make one of these mandarin-style collars. Lay the pattern piece for the collar on a flat surface.

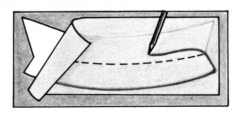

1 Trace the lower edge as far as the foldline, then draw a line $\frac{5}{8}$in (1.5cm) above the foldline.

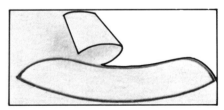

2 Cut out the traced pattern. Mark $\frac{5}{8}$in (1.5cm) seam allowance on all sides and add any pattern markings.

Smocked dress

This softly smocked dress is adapted from the pattern for the basic shirt. It would be a very versatile addition to your wardrobe—and would make a pretty maternity dress.

Kim Sayer

Altering the pattern

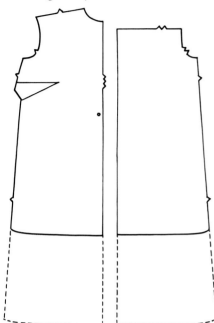

1 Decide how long you would like the finished dress to be.

Using the shirt pattern from the Stitch by Stitch Pattern Pack, trace the front and back pieces, leaving enough paper at the hem edge to extend the pattern to the finished length. Continue the center back, center front and side edges down to the required length.

2 Draw the hemline on each piece. Check the length at intervals by measuring down from the shirt hemline to make sure it is even. Add a 2½in (6.5cm) hem allowance below the hemline. Cut out the front pattern piece only.

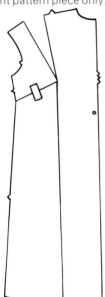

Terry Evans

3 On the shirt front draw a line down the pattern parallel to the center front, passing through the bust dart point.

Materials
3 sheets of tracing paper at least 48x24in (120x60cm) (join smaller pieces if necessary)

4 Slash along the line from the upper edge (yoke line) to the dart point. Close the dart and tape in place. The slash will open.

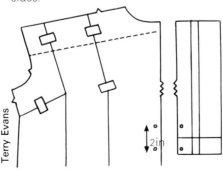

5 Slash down the remainder of the line so that the pattern is in two parts. Lay the pieces on a sheet of paper and spread them so that they are 8⅝in (22cm) apart below the bust point. Tape the pieces to the paper, first checking that the pattern is square by making sure the line for lengthening or shortening is level on both sides.

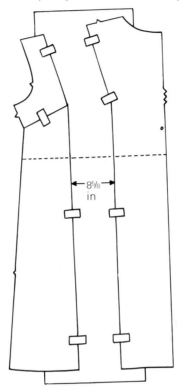

6 Re-draw the upper cutting line by joining the neck corner and top armhole edge as shown. Mark the seam allowance ⅝in (1.5cm) down from the cutting line.
7 At the center front re-draw the circle for the finished length of the front band (marked "clip"), placing it 2in (5cm)

higher than the original circle. Cut off 2in (5cm) from the lower edge of the front band to correspond.
8 Measure down 2⅜in (6cm) from yoke seamline on the pattern front and draw a line parallel to the seamline to mark the finished depth of the smocking.

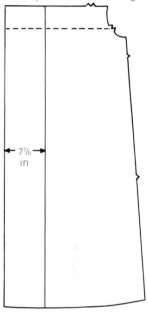

9 On the dress back piece, draw a vertical line 7⅞in (20cm) outside center back line to allow extra fullness for smocking. Mark this as the foldline. Measure down 2⅜in (6cm) from the yoke seamline and mark off the depth of the smocking.

Directions for making

Measurements
The pattern is given in sizes 10, 12, 14, 16, 18 and 20, corresponding to sizes 8 to 18 in ready-made clothes.

Suggested fabrics
Soft fabrics such as wool or crepe, Viyella®, cotton and wool blends, challis, lightweight flannel, single knits.

Materials
45in (115cm)-wide fabric with or without nap:
  Sizes 10, 12, 14: 4yd (3.6m)
  Sizes 16, 18, 20: 4⅛yd (3.7m)
54in (140cm)-wide fabric with or without nap:
  Sizes 10, 12, 14: 3⅝yd (3.3m)
  Sizes 16, 18, 20: 3¾yd (3.4m)
45in (115cm)-wide lining fabric:
  For all sizes: 2⅞yd (2.6m)
36in (90cm)-wide interfacing:
  For all sizes: ½yd (.4m)
Matching thread
Cotton embroidery floss or pearl cotton for smocking
Smocking dot transfers
2½in (1.3cm)-diameter buttons

45in-(115cm-)wide fabric with or without nap

fold

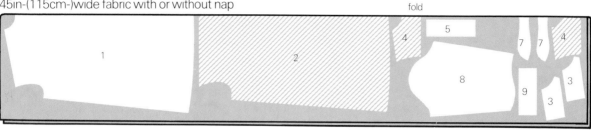

selvages

54in-(140cm-)wide fabric with or without nap

fold

fold

Interfacing
36in-(90cm-)
wide fabric

selvages

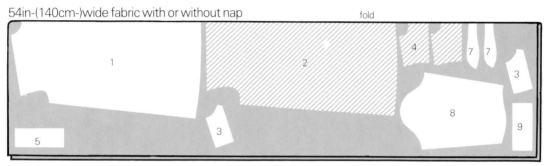

Key to adjusted pattern pieces

1 Dress front	Cut 1 on fold
2 Dress back	Cut 1 on fold
3 Front yoke	Cut 4
4 Back yoke	Cut 2 on fold
5 Front band	Cut 2
7 Collar band	Cut 2 on fold
8 Sleeve	Cut 2
9 Cuff	Cut 2

Lining: use pieces 1 and 2.
Interfacing: use pieces 5, 7 and 9.

1 Alter the pattern pieces for the dress front, dress back and front band as directed on page 54.
2 Prepare the main fabric and pin on the pattern pieces, following the layout for your fabric width. Cut out the pieces, following the outline of the pattern closely.
3 Transfer the markings from the pattern to the fabric and remove the pattern pieces.
4 Fold the lining fabric in half and pin on the pattern pieces for the dress front and back, placing center front and center back on fold. Cut out the pattern pieces and transfer the markings from the pattern to the fabric.
5 Cut a length of smocking dots, six dots deep, to fit the areas to be smocked on the dress back and front. Place the dots in the areas marked, making sure they do not overlap the seam allowances. Press the transfer with a hot iron and run lines of gathering for the pleats as shown in Volume 6, page 78. Draw up and fasten threads.

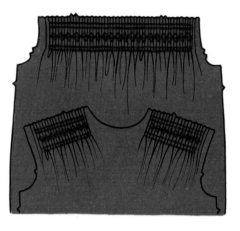

6 Make one row of double cable stitch, one row of Vandyke stitch, and another row of double cable stitch over the pleats on the dress back and front (see Volume 6, pages 78-79). Press smocking on wrong side and remove the gathering threads.

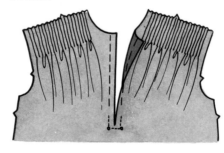

7 Staystitch around the bottom inner corners of the front opening and slash down the center front fold line to within $\frac{5}{8}$in (1.5cm) of horizontal line of stitching on dress and lining. Baste dress front and front lining together at center front on the seamline for the front band.

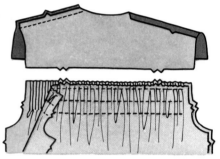

8 Interface and attach the front bands to dress as shown in Volume 5, pages 57-58. (This shortened band has no buttonholes or buttons.)
9 Baste and sew the yoke back and fronts together with right sides facing. Stitch together the yoke back and fronts for the yoke facing in the same way.
10 Run gathering stitches on the yoke seamlines of the dress lining back and front. Add another row of gathering stitches, $\frac{7}{8}$in (2.3cm) from seamline and another, $\frac{7}{8}$in (2.3cm) below that. Pull up all gathering stitches until the lining fits the smocked area, and fasten.

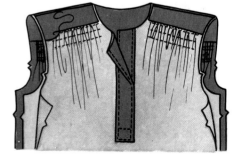

11 Baste and sew the yoke to the dress front and back, including the lining in the

seams. Grade the seams and press up.
12 Baste the yoke facings to the yoke at the neck and armhole edges and turn under and slip stitch the seam allowances along the yoke seam lines.

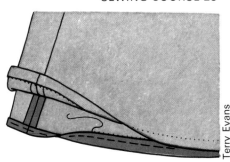

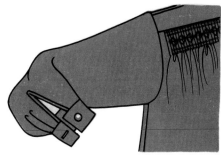

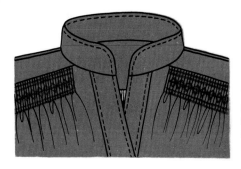

13 Make and attach the collar band to the neck edge as shown on page 53.

16 Run a line of gathering around both sleeve caps; baste and sew the sleeves into the armholes. Finish the seams. Make a buttonhole on each cuff and sew a button to the other edge of each cuff to correspond.

17 Try on the dress and mark the hemline. Turn up the hem and baste close to the folded edge. Trim the hem allowance to an even depth and turn under $\frac{1}{4}$in (6mm) at the raw edge. Hem the dress and press the folded edge only.
Repeat with the hem of the lining, making it $\frac{5}{8}$in (1.5cm) shorter than the dress.

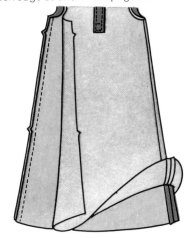

14 Baste and sew the side seams of the dress, placing right sides together, keeping the lining free. Press open and finish. Baste and sew the side seams of the lining together. Press seams open and finish.

15 Stitch the side seams of the sleeves with right sides together. Make a continuous lap opening for the slash in each sleeve. Interface the cuffs and attach them to the sleeves (see Volume 5, page 63). The sleeves are not lined.

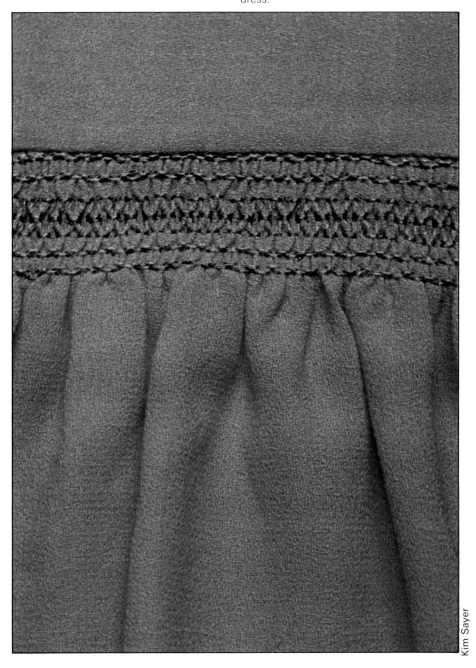

Terry Evans

Kim Sayer

57

*Hand-rolled hems
*Applying circular collar
 with binding
* Evening dress: adapting the
 pattern; directions for making
 (1)

Hand-rolled hems

A hand-rolled hem makes a delicate finish on sheer fabrics such as chiffon, crepe, lace and organza. This type of hem is usually used on silk scarves, as well as on evening and wedding gowns made from sheet fabrics. It is particularly useful on widely flared garments where a large part of the hem edge is on the bias, as it eliminates the problem of easing the hem allowance in place.

There are two methods of forming a rolled hem. One method produces a plain rolled hem on which the stitches are invisible on the right side. In the other method, stitches are taken over the hem and pulled up to form tiny scallops; this kind of rolled hem is called a shell edging. The preparation is the same for both kinds of hem; neither should be pressed.

Plain rolled hem

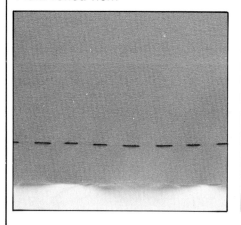

1 If the hem is on a dress, mark the hemline with a row of basting (after allowing the dress to hang for a few days).

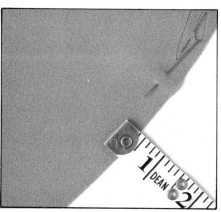

2 In other cases—for example, the circular collar on the dress on page 61—measure from the cutting line to determine the position of the hem.

3 Add a line of machine stitching $\frac{1}{8}$in (3mm) below the hemline, using a short stitch length. Check the tension on a scrap of fabric first. Trim away the hem allowance $\frac{1}{8}$in (3mm) below line of machine stitching. The stitches help prevent the hem from raveling. Press.

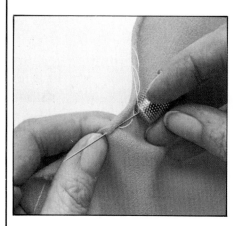

4 Roll the edge of the fabric to the wrong side, using the thumb and forefinger of the left hand. Check that the stitches do not show. Using a fine needle and thread and working from right to left, take a stitch through the fold of the fabric.

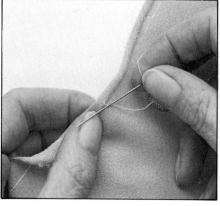

5 Then take the needle diagonally to the left and take a stitch in the fabric $\frac{1}{8}$in (3mm) in from the basted hemline. Catch only a single thread so that the stitches do not show on the right side.

6 Continue in this way around the hem edge, drawing the stitches down at regular intervals to form a neatly rolled hem.

Shell edging

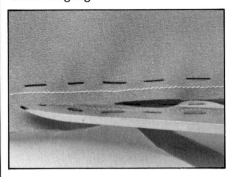 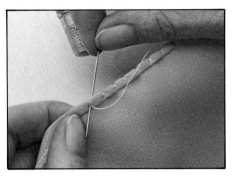 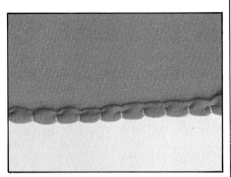

1 Prepare the hem with basting and machine stitches as described in step 3 under "Plain rolled hem." Trim away the hem allowance $\frac{1}{8}$in (3mm) outside the machine stitches.

2 Fold the hem edge to the wrong side. Anchor the thread on the wrong side and take the needle over the fold of the hem as shown and into the right side of the fabric, $\frac{1}{8}$in (3mm) from fold. Bring thread through to wrong side, then make another stitch in the same way, over the first. Pull the thread to gather up hem fold.

3 Take the needle to the left, running it through the fold. Make another double stitch over the edge, and pull up the thread to form a scallop. Continue in this way, spacing the stitches at regular intervals. The distance between stitches is usually $\frac{1}{4}-\frac{3}{8}$in (6-10mm).

Circular collar with binding

This soft, pretty collar could be used to add a flattering touch to a blouse or dress with a plain neck. It could also substitute for a shirt collar.

For the step-by-step directions here, we have made a double circular collar like the one on the dress shown on page 61. For a single collar, the procedure is essentially the same.

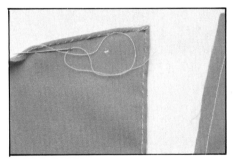 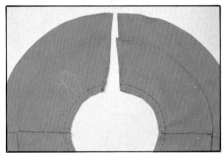

1 Cut out the circle to the required diameter, adding $\frac{5}{8}$in (1.5cm) to outer and neckline edges. The circles used here measure $8\frac{3}{4}$in (22.5cm) and 11in (28cm), and the neck opening (unfinished) is 4in (10cm) in diameter. Mark center back and shoulder points on collars with lines of basting. Slash down center front. Finish outer edge with a hand-rolled hem.

2 Baste the two collar pieces together around the neck edge with right sides up. (For this style the front opening is finished before the collar is applied.) Run two rows of gathering stitches at the neck edge, one row $\frac{1}{8}$in (3mm) inside seamline and the other $\frac{1}{8}$in (3mm) outside the seamline.

3 Pin the collars, right side up, to the right side of the dress, matching the center back and front on the collars to those on the dress. Match the shoulder points to the shoulder seams. Pull up the gathers. Baste in place on seamline.

4 Measure around the neck edge and add $1\frac{1}{8}$in (3cm) to this measurement. Cut a bias strip $1\frac{3}{8}$in (3.5cm) wide by the length just measured, to bind neck. Baste binding to neck edge, right sides together. Stitch $\frac{5}{8}$in (1.5cm) from edge.

5 Trim seams to $\frac{1}{4}$in (6mm) and press binding over seam allowances to inside of neck. Turn in short ends of bias strip, then fold under $\frac{1}{4}$in (6mm) on long edge. Baste and slip stitch in place.

Mike Berend

Something special

This lovely evening dress, which begins here and is finished in the next Sewing course, is made by adapting the pattern for the basic dress in the Pattern Pack. The simple lines are enhanced by the flowing, silky fabric.

Adapting the pattern

Materials
3 sheets of tracing paper 63 x 18in (160 x 45cm)
Ruler
Compass

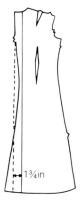

1 Trace the front and back pattern pieces. On the dress back tracing, extend the grain line to the neck and hem edges of the pattern. Draw another line parallel to the grain line and $1\frac{3}{4}$in (4.5cm) outside it to straighten the center back line. Mark this as the foldline.

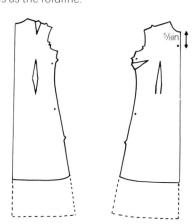

2 Decide on the finished dress length needed, measuring from the back neck. Extend the front and back dress pieces to this length, plus $\frac{5}{8}$in (1.5cm) hem allowance, to carry down the original hemline on the pattern.
3 Mark the top of the zipper $1\frac{3}{8}$in (3.5cm) below the armhole on the side seamline,

and mark the zipper base 14in (35.5cm) below the first point.
4 Measure down 6in (15cm) at the center front and mark the position for the bottom of the front opening.

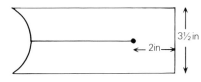

5 On a separate piece of paper draw a rectangle 9in (22.5cm) long and $3\frac{1}{2}$in (9cm) wide. Draw a line lengthwise down the center of the rectangle, stopping 2in (5cm) from one edge. Place the rectangle over the dress front edge, and trace the neck curve on one side. Reverse the paper and draw in the curve on the other side. This is the neck facing pattern.

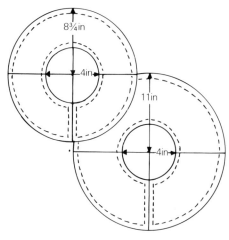

6 Using the compass, draw a 4in (10cm)-diameter circle on a new sheet of paper. Draw a concentric circle with a radius of $8\frac{3}{4}$in (22cm) outside the first. This is the pattern for the top collar. Draw a pattern for the lower collar the same way, giving the outer circle a radius of 11in (28cm). Both pieces have $\frac{5}{8}$in (1.5cm) seam allowances on each edge.
7 Draw a line through the center of the circle and mark two points for center front and back. Holding a ruler at 90 degrees to this line, mark two points for shoulder seam positions.

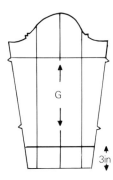

8 Trace sleeve pattern, and extend cuff edge by 3in (7.5cm). Divide the width

Terry Evans

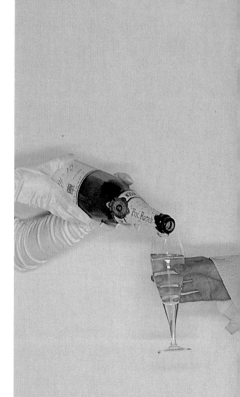

Change the look of the dress completely by using a different fabric for the collars—here the effect you can achieve with a boldly contrasting color is shown. Or try binding the collar in another fabric to emphasize the edges. This version takes 16in (40cm) of contrasting fabric; draw a revised cutting layout before buying the fabric to avoid waste.

Victor Yuan

Terry Evans

of the cuff edge into four equal parts. Draw a horizontal line joining the upper notches on the side edges, and divide this line into four equal sections. Draw three straight lines joining each pair of marks.

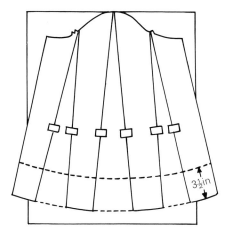

9 Slash along these three lines up to the seamline on the sleeve. Open each slash at bottom edge by $3\frac{1}{8}$in (8cm) and tape paper under each slash. Re-draw the lower edge. Mark a new grain line through the center of the sleeve.

10 Measure across the sleeve at intervals $3\frac{1}{2}$in (9cm) from lower edge. Connect marks for the casing position.

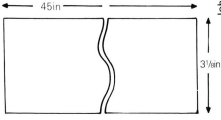

11 Draw a rectangle measuring 45in (115cm) long and $3\frac{1}{8}$in (8cm) wide for belt. This includes $\frac{5}{8}$in (1.5cm) seam allowances on both edges. Draw the straight grain line parallel to one edge.

Directions for making (1)

Measurements

The pattern is given in sizes 10, 12, 14, 16, 18 and 20, corresponding to size 8 to 18 in ready-made clothes.

Suggested fabrics

Soft fabrics such as crepe, crepe de chine, wool challis, single knits.

Materials

45 or 54in (115 or 140cm)-wide fabric with or without nap:
Sizes 10, 12, 14: $4\frac{3}{8}$yd (4.5m)
Sizes 16, 18, 20: $4\frac{1}{2}$yd (4.6m)
14in (35.5cm) dress zipper
One $\frac{1}{4}$in (6mm) button; thread
16in (40cm) of $\frac{1}{4}$in (6mm)-wide elastic

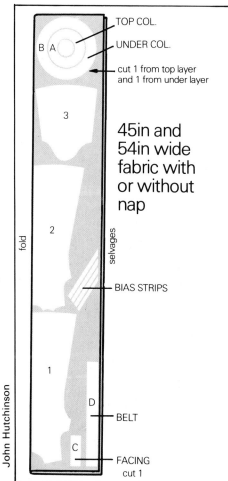

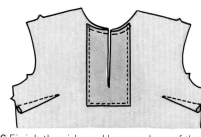

45in and 54in wide fabric with or without nap

BIAS STRIPS
BELT
FACING
cut 1

Key to adjusted pattern pieces

1	Dress front	Cut 1 on fold
2	Dress back	Cut 1 on fold
3	Sleeve	Cut 2
A	Top collar	Cut 1
B	Lower collar	Cut 1
C	Front facing	Cut 1
D	Belt	Cut 2

1 Alter the pattern pieces for the dress front, back and sleeve and draw the additional pattern pieces (see page 60).
2 Prepare the fabric and pin on the pattern pieces as shown on the cutting layout. Make sure that the grain lines on the pattern lie on the straight grain of the fabric. Cut out pieces. From remaining fabric cut enough bias strips $1\frac{1}{8}$in (3cm) wide, to form a piece $19\frac{1}{2}$in (50cm) long.
3 Transfer the markings from the pattern to the fabric and remove pattern pieces.

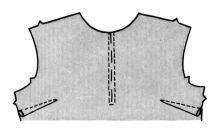

4 Fold, baste and sew the bust and waist darts on the dress front and the shoulder

and waist darts on the dress back. Press the waist and shoulder darts toward the center back and bust darts down.
5 Mark the center front opening with basting, and stay-stitch around the bottom of the opening.

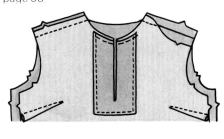

6 Finish the side and lower edges of the front facing. Apply the front facing to the dress front with right sides together as shown in Sewing course 5, Volume 1, page 58.

7 Baste and sew the shoulder seams with right sides together. Press the seams open and finish.

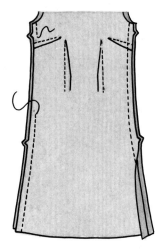

8 Slash the center front of both collars. Finish outer edges and center fronts with a hand-rolled hem. Attach collars to neck and bind as on page 59.

9 Baste and sew the side seams, leaving the left seam open for the zipper between the dots. Press seams open and finish.

Shoeshine bag

Keep all your shoe-cleaning gear together in this neat roll-up holdall.

Finished size
9½in (24cm) long
¾in (2cm) seam allowance is included.

Materials
½yd (.4m) of 36in (90cm)-wide striped cotton fabric
⅜yd (.3m) of 36in (90cm)-wide heavyweight interfacing
Piece of stiff cardboard 6¼×3⅛in (16×8cm)
Matching sewing thread
Two snaps

1 From cotton fabric cut out two main pieces each 14×11in (36×28cm). For ends cut out four 3¾in (9.5cm)-diameter circles.
2 From interfacing cut out one piece the same size as the main fabric piece.
3 From cardboard cut out two 3in (7.5cm)-diameter circles for end pieces.
4 Place fabric circles in pairs with wrong sides together. Pin, baste and stitch around each pair, leaving an opening large enough for cardboard circles.
5 Trim and turn both fabric circles right side out. Insert cardboard circles, turn in opening edges and slip stitch together to close.
6 Round off both corners on one short side of each main fabric piece. Repeat on interfacing piece.
7 Place main fabric pieces together with wrong sides facing. Place interfacing on one side of fabric pieces. Pin, baste and stitch together all around, leaving a 3⅛in (8cm) opening in one short side. Trim and turn main piece right side out.
Turn in opening edges and slip stitch together to close.
8 Topstitch all around main piece, ⅜in (1cm) from outer edge.
9 Position one covered circle at edge of one long side of main piece. Slip stitch circle to main piece around outer edge, leaving about one-third of circle free at top.
10 Repeat step 9 to stitch the second fabric circle in the same position on the opposite long side.
11 Sew top halves of two snaps to holdall, 5½in (14cm) apart and 1½in (4cm) from top short edge. Sew opposite halves of snaps to opposite short side to correspond.

Paul Williams

Inserting a zipper in a side seam by the lapped seam method

This method of inserting a zipper is used where the zipper falls in the middle of a seam, such as the side seam of a dress. The finished effect is similar to that of the lapped seam method described in Sewing course 7, Volume 2, page 45.

The method shown here can also be used for an open-ended skirt zipper by stitching along the sides and lower edge of the zipper only.

When in place, the zipper is well-hidden by the seam allowance, but if you want to make it even more inconspicuous you can sew the final topstitching by hand.

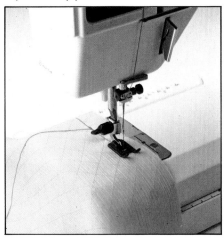

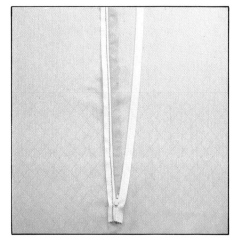

1 Close the zipper opening in the left side seam of the garment with machine basting, using the longest stitch on the machine. Press the seam open. (This step can be included when you stitch the side seam, but remember to secure the stitching at both ends of the opening by stitching backward and forward using the regular length stitch.)

2 Working on the inside of the dress, open the zipper and place the right-hand tape face down on the back seam allowance with the teeth on the seamline and the bottom of the zipper at the bottom of the opening.

Attach the zipper foot to the machine so that the needle is to the left of the foot. Baste the zipper to the seam allowance only, then stitch from bottom to top, sewing close to the zipper teeth.

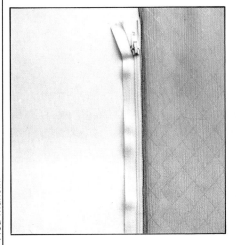

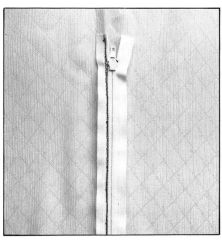

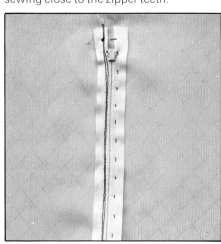

3 Close the zipper. Still working on the inside of the dress, press the fabric away from the teeth. With needle to right of foot, stitch from the bottom of the zipper to the top close to the fold, through seam allowance and tape only.

4 Place the zipper flat against the seam so that the unstitched tape lies over the front seam allowance. There will be a small pleat at the top and bottom of the zipper tape already stitched.

5 Pin the front zipper tape in position, through both the seam allowance and garment front. Baste $\frac{3}{8}$in (1cm) from the fold and across the top and bottom ends of the zipper tape.

Fred Mancini

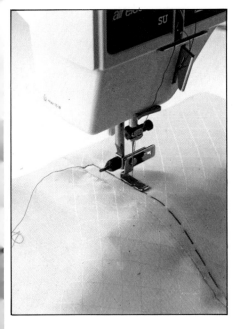

6 Sew the zipper in place by machine or by hand, working from the right side of the garment and using the basting as a guide.
Anchor the threads on the inside of the seam and remove basting and machine basting. Press carefully, taking care—if you are using a nylon zipper—not to place the iron over the teeth.

7 A zipper finished by hand-picking. (See Sewing course 7, Volume 2, page 46.)

8 This picture shows the finished effect when the zipper is stitched by machine.

Sleeve casing with elastic

A casing threaded with elastic is a very simple and neat way of controlling the fullness at the wrist edge of a sleeve. Because the elastic stretches when you put on the garment, no wrist opening is necessary. This feature makes a garment easy to put on and take off, and for this reason it is often used on babies' and children's clothes.
The casing is attached to the sleeve after the sleeve has been sewn and the lower edge has been finished.
The casing can be made either from straight seam binding or from a strip of the same fabric as the garment.

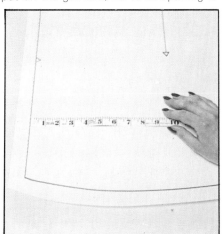

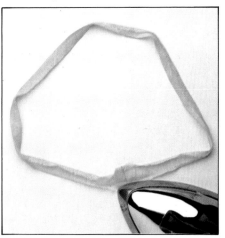

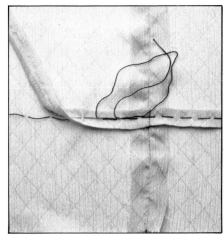

1 Measure across the casing position on the sleeve pattern (including the seam allowances) to determine the length of binding required. If you are using the garment fabric, cut the binding 1 in (2.5cm) wide.

2 Press under ¼in (6mm) on wrong side along both edges of binding. Join the two short ends of the strip with right sides together, to form a circle. Press the seam open.

3 Pin and baste the binding to the sleeve, centering it over the line for the casing position and making sure the wrong sides are together. The seam in the casing should fall at the sleeve seam.

continued

Fred Mancini

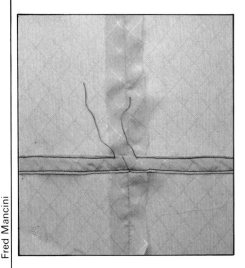

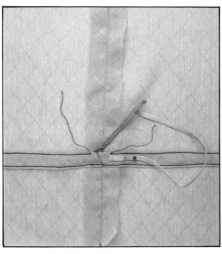

4 Sew the binding in place along both edges, close to the edge, leaving a $\frac{5}{8}$in (1.5cm)-long opening in the upper edge at the sleeve seam. Press.

5 Cut a piece of elastic to fit the wrist comfortably plus $\frac{3}{4}$in (2cm) for joining. Secure one end of the elastic at the casing opening with a pin and thread the other end through the binding using a safety pin or bodkin. This will gather up the sleeve fabric to fit the wrist.

6 Pin ends of elastic together and slip sleeve over wrist. Adjust elastic if necessary. Sew the elastic ends together firmly and push the elastic back into the casing. Slip stitch the opening in the casing.

Thread loops

Thread loops are usually used as button fastenings on openings where there is no overlap of fabric. They are most often used at the neck edge of evening wear, on blouses made of sheer fabrics and on lingerie.

On convertible necklines which can be worn buttoned up, a thread loop is often used for the top button so that the fastening is inconspicuous when the collar is worn open.

Thread loops can also be used in place of metal eyes for hooks, usually at the back neck above a zipper.

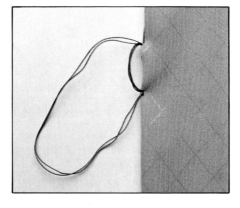

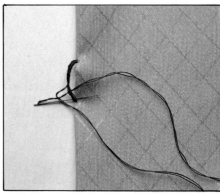

1 Using the thread double, take two back stitches on the inside of the garment at the position for the top of the loop. Bring the needle to the right side and take the thread to the position for the bottom of the loop. Leave the loop slightly slack and if the loop is for a button fastening, check that the button fits. Take two more stitches in the same way so that the foundation loop has six strands.

2 Sew over the loops with blanket stitches, as shown. Continue working in this way until the loop is tightly covered with stitches. Take the thread through to the wrong side and secure the ends with two back stitches.

Thread belt carriers

Belt carriers are used to hold a belt in place at the waistline of a garment. Thread belt carriers are less conspicuous than those made of fabric, and for this reason they are often used on dresses.

Thread loops should be $\frac{1}{4}$in (6mm) longer than the width of the belt so that the belt slips easily into the carrier but should not be so long that the belt will hang below the waist.

There are two kinds of belt carriers: one is simply a thread loop, made large enough to accommodate the belt (see above); the other is produced by sewing a chain, as shown on page 67.

Thread chain belt carrier

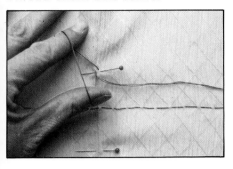 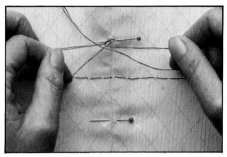 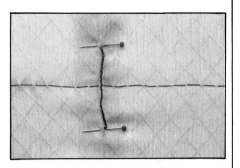

1 With pins, mark the position for the belt carriers above and below the belt line. Take two small back stitches on the wrong side of the garment at the upper pin. Take the thread through the fabric to the right side.

2 Take a small stitch in the fabric, and pull the thread part of the way through, leaving a small loop. Drop the needle and, holding the loop with one hand, pull free thread through with the other hand, forming a new loop. Slip the first loop off your fingers and pull the new loop gently to tighten the chain.

3 Continue pulling the thread through each new loop until chain is desired length. Then take needle through loop and pull to form a knot. Take needle to the wrong side of the fabric at the place marked by the lower pin and sew two back stitches to anchor the thread. If you prefer, you can make a length of chain to go completely around the belt and attach both ends at the waistline.

Long evening dress: directions for making (2)

Directions for finishing the long evening dress. It is made in cotton and decorated with a colorful scarf.

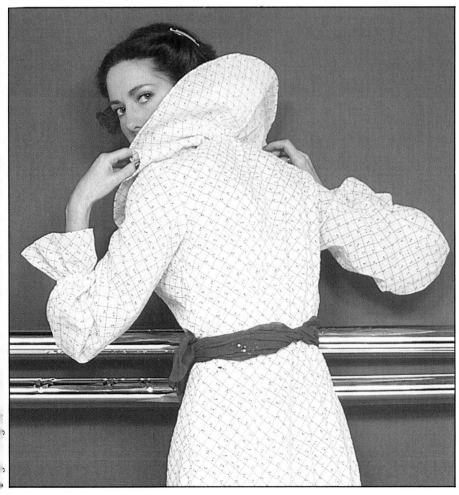

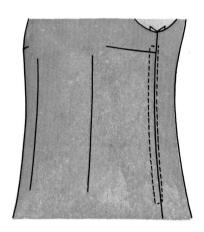

1 Insert the zipper into the opening in the left side seam using the lapped seam method shown on page 64.

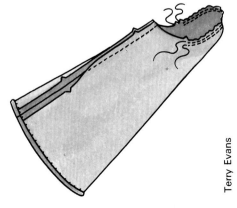

2 Run two rows of gathering stitches between the notches on the sleeve cap. Baste and sew the underarm seam of the sleeve with right sides together and

Terry Evans

notches matching. Press the seam open and finish it. Finish the lower edge of the sleeve using a plain hand-rolled hem or shell edging (see pages 58-59).

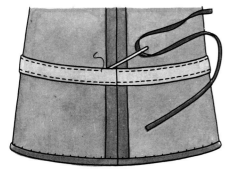

3 From remaining fabric cut two strips 19½ by 1in (50 by 2.5cm) for casings. Press under ¼in (6mm) on wrong side along both long edges of each strip. Join short ends of each strip to form two rings and attach the casings to the sleeve as shown on pages 65-66. Insert elastic to fit your wrist and fasten ends firmly.

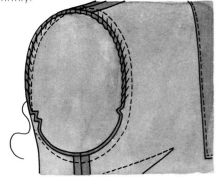

4 Baste and sew the sleeve into the armhole, distributing the ease evenly. Press the seam allowances and finish by overcasting them together.
5 Try on the dress and mark the finished length. Turn up the hem using a hand-rolled hem or shell edging as shown on pages 58-59.

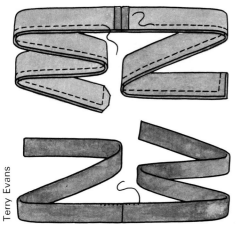

6 Baste and sew the two belt sections together along one short edge, right sides together. Press the seam open. Fold the

belt in half lengthwise with right sides together and raw edges matching. Baste along all raw edges. Stitch these three sides of the belt, leaving an opening 6in (15cm) long in the center of the long side. Trim the seam allowances, cut across the corners and turn the belt right side out. Fold in the raw edges of the opening and baste all around the stitched edges, taking the stitching to the outer edge. Slip stitch opening. Press the belt.

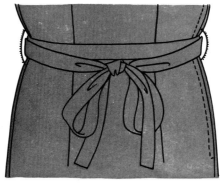

7 Try on the dress again and mark the position of the belt carriers ⅝in (1.5cm) above and below the belt line on both side seams. Sew thread belt carriers in positions marked, using either the blanket stitch method (see page 66) or the chain method (see page 67). Make a thread loop for the button fastening at the right-hand side of the neck binding. Sew the button onto the left-hand side of the binding.

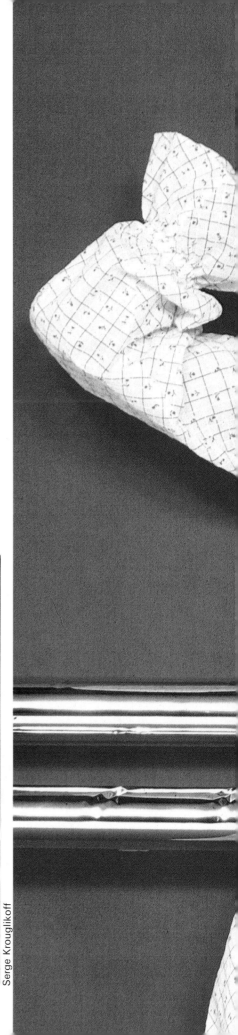

Terry Evans

Serge Krouglikoff

68

*Working with unbalanced
  plaid fabrics
*Split darts
*Using wool braid
*Long vest:
  adapting the pattern;
  directions for making

Working with unbalanced plaid fabrics

An unbalanced plaid fabric is one in which the plaids do not run the same in both directions; that is, the plaids may be rectangular instead of square, or there may be an irregular stripe incorporated into the design.

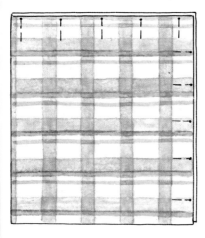

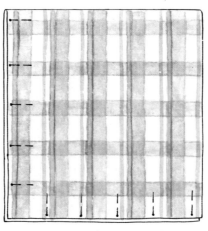

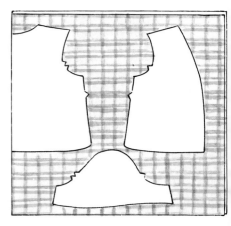

1 Plaids are unbalanced lengthwise if the stripes running perpendicular to the selvage are uneven—that is, the plaids don't form a mirror image on each side of a central stripe. Fold the fabric parallel to the selvage with right sides together, so that the center of a plaid or stripe lies along the fold. Match the top and bottom layers together exactly and pin.

2 Plaids are unbalanced crosswise if the stripes running parallel to the selvage are uneven. They can be matched only if the pattern has a center seam or opening in the front or back. Fold the fabric perpendicular to the selvage, match the top and bottom layers together exactly and pin.

3 The pattern pieces must be laid on the fabric in the same direction, regardless of whether the fabric is unbalanced lengthwise or crosswise. Notches which will be matched together must be placed on the same stripe. Remember that the plaids must be matched on the seamline and not the cutting line.

Plaids unbalanced in both directions

If the fabric is unbalanced in both directions—that is, when the stripes of the plaid are irregular in both directions—the plaids can be matched only when the fabric has no right or wrong side, as the fabric pieces must be reversed when cutting out. When the pieces are seamed, one section is simply reversed; as there is no right or wrong side to the fabric, both pieces are identical. Be sure to slip-baste all seams when making the garment so that the matched areas do not slip out of alignment (see Volume 6, page 69).

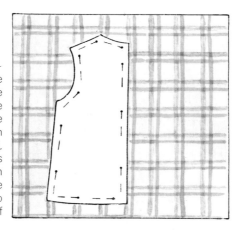

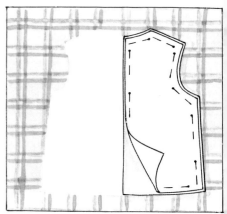

1 Lay the fabric flat with the right side facing up. Place the pattern pieces on the fabric in one direction only, with the center seam on a prominent lengthwise stripe. Cut out the pattern pieces.

2 When cutting out the second set of pattern pieces, use those you have already cut out, placing them right side down on the fabric and matching the plaids together on both pieces.

Split darts

A split dart is stitched in the same way as a normal dart but is slashed along the foldline and pressed open. This type of dart is used on thick fabrics such as tweed and flannel to reduce the thickness when the dart is pressed and to prevent a ridge from showing on the right side.

1 Fold, baste and sew the dart in the normal way, from the widest end to the point. Secure the threads and press the dart away from the garment, so that the garment does not lie beneath the dart.

2 Slash along the center fold to within 1in (2.5cm) of the dart point. Press the dart open and the point flat.
If the fabric ravels badly, overcast the raw edges of the dart. If the fabric does not ravel, the dart edges may be left unfinished.

Using braid trim

Braid can be used either to bind a raw edge or as a purely decorative feature on a garment. It is usually applied to the collar, cuff, lapel, pocket or outer edge of a garment.
The type of braid used for this kind of finish is woven on the bias so that it can be fitted easily around curved edges. The braid is sold either flat or folded. Folded braid is usually pressed in half, or is pressed slightly off center so that the lower edge is marginally wider than the top edge. When the braid is stitched on from the top, the lower edge is easily included in the stitching.

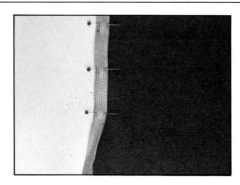

1 If a seam allowance has been included on the edge to be bound, trim away the fabric on the seam line.
If the braid is not already folded, press it so that the lower edge is $\frac{1}{8}$in (3mm) wider than the top edge. Place the wider edge on the wrong side of the fabric so that the raw edge of the garment lies between the two edges.

2 Baste the braid in place and sew close to the inner edge, working from the right side of the garment.

Mitered corners on braid edging

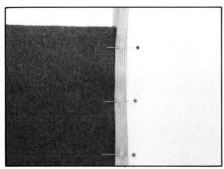

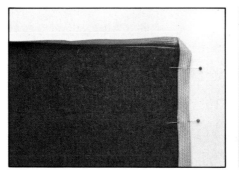

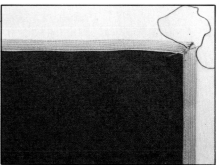

1 If a seam allowance has been included, trim away the fabric on the seamline. Pin the braid in place as far as the corner.

2 Working from the right side, open out the folded braid and place the foldline exactly at the corner of the fabric. Continue positioning the braid along the next edge, also with the raw edge of the fabric to the fold. Pin in place. Press a diagonal crease in the braid at the corner.

3 Fold the braid over onto the fabric and pin in place. Repeat this on the wrong side.
Sew the binding in place close to the inner edge, working from the right side. Slip stitch the miter in place along the small folds and press.

Paul Williams

Miter and tie fastening

A miter and tie fastening is usually made from braid, leather or suede. It consists of the miter, made by folding the braid into a triangular shape, and a tie end, which is held securely in place by the miter.

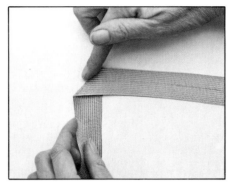

1 Lay the braid flat and fold the top end down to the right so that an exactly diagonal fold is made.

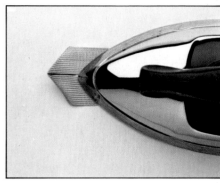

2 Bring the bottom end up and over to the right so that the sides of the braid meet at the center and a point is formed at the left as shown. Press the miter flat.

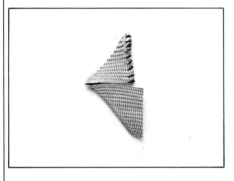

3 Cut off long ends, ¼in (6mm) beyond straight bottom layer of the miter. Turn in the ends and slip stitch them in place. If you are using leather or suede, these edges can be left flat and cut off in line with the bottom layer of the miter.

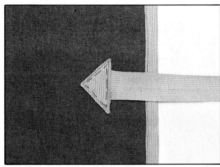

4 Cut a piece of braid long enough for the fastening and pin it in place on the front of the garment. Place the miter over the end of the tie with the straight edge at the center of the garment; baste down. Sew around all three edges. Press.

5 Make another miter and tie fastening in the same way for the other side of the garment. Attach it opposite the first.

Long vest

This versatile vest will give a new look to a blouse and skirt. It's very quick and easy to make.

Adapting the pattern

Measurements

The vest is made by adapting the pattern for the jacket from the Stitch by Stitch Pattern Pack, available in sizes 10-20, which correspond to sizes 8-18 in ready-made clothes.

Note ⅝in (1.5cm) seam allowances are included throughout.

Materials

Sheets of tracing paper at least 30 x 15in (76 x 38cm)
Flexible curve

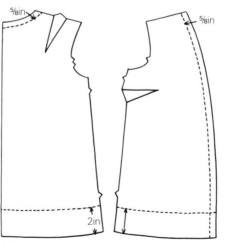

1 Trace the front and back pieces for the jacket. If a longer vest is required, extend the side, center back and center front edges down to the length needed. If a shorter vest is required, shorten the pattern on the lines indicated on the pattern.
Trim away the seam allowance on the back neck edge and down front edge, ⅝in (1.5cm) from cutting line. Trim away

hem edge on the foldline, 2in (5cm) from cutting line on both front and back pattern pieces. The front, neck, armhole and hem edges of the vest are bound.

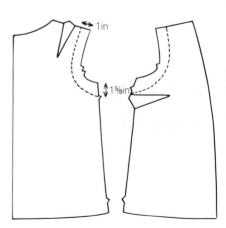

2 On both pattern pieces mark a point 1in (2.5cm) from armhole edge at shoulder. Mark a point 1⅝in (4cm) from cutting line at underarm. Join the two points with a flexible curve to form the new armhole cutting line.

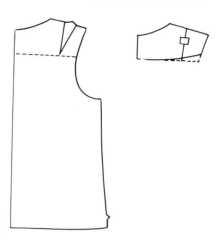

pattern pack

3 Draw a line at right angles to the center back, in line with the shoulder dart point. Cut along this line to separate the back yoke from the bodice.
Tape the dart in place on the yoke. Straighten the lower edge of the yoke where the dart has curved the pattern upward. Add $\frac{5}{8}$in (1.5cm) for seams to cut edges of yoke and bodice.

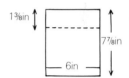

4 Draw a rectangle 6in (15.5cm) by $7\frac{7}{8}$in (20cm) for pocket. Draw facing fold line $1\frac{3}{8}$in (3.5cm) from top.

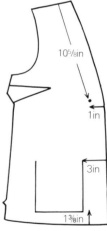

5 On the front pattern piece, measure up $1\frac{3}{8}$in (3.5cm) from lower edge and 3in (7.5cm) in from center front edge. Mark this point, which is the position of the inner corner of the pocket. Measure in 3in (7.5cm) from center front, $6\frac{1}{2}$in (16.5cm) above first mark for the top corner of the pocket. Connect the two points. Draw the other pocket edge 6in (15.5cm) away from that line. Measure $10\frac{5}{8}$in (27cm) along the front neck edge from the shoulder and mark this point. Measure in 1in (2.5cm) from this point and mark the position of the miter and tie fastening.

Directions for making

Suggested fabrics
Wool flannel, wool tweed, corduroy or quilted cotton.

Materials
These yardages are for a vest the same length as the original jacket pattern piece. If you choose to lengthen or shorten it, check to see if you need to buy more or less fabric.

45in (115cm)-wide fabric, with or without nap: all sizes: 1½yd (1.3m)
54in (140cm)-wide fabric, with or without nap: sizes 10-16: 1⅛yd (1m), sizes 18, 20: 1⅓yd (1.2m)
Matching thread; 5½yd (5.3m) of 1⅛in (3cm)-wide braid

Key to adjusted pattern pieces:
1 Vest front
2 Vest back
A Back yoke
B Pocket

1 Alter the pattern pieces for the vest front and back, and draw the pocket as shown on pages 72-73.
2 Prepare the fabric and pin on the four pattern pieces following the correct layout for your fabric width. If you are using an unbalanced plaid fabric, follow the directions on page 70.
3 Transfer all pattern markings.

Cutting layout

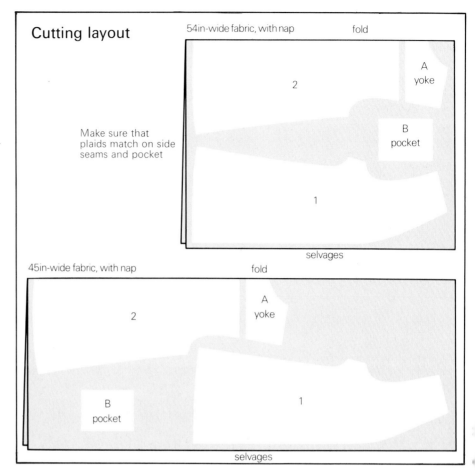

Make sure that plaids match on side seams and pocket

54in-wide fabric, with nap — fold
2
A yoke
B pocket
1
selvages

45in-wide fabric, with nap — fold
2
A yoke
B pocket
1
selvages

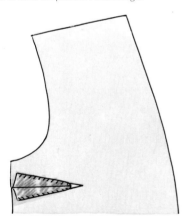

4 Pin, baste and sew the split bust darts as shown on page 71.

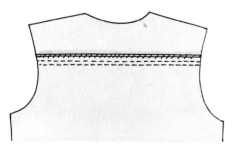

5 Baste and sew the back yoke to the vest back, matching the pattern if you use a plaid fabric. Overcast the seams together and press up. Topstitch ¼in (6mm) from the seam line on the right side of the yoke. Press.

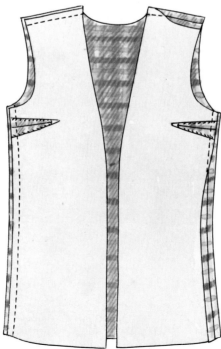

6 Baste and sew the shoulder and side seams using slip-basting on plaid fabrics to ensure that the pattern will match.

Finish the seam allowances with machine zig-zag stitches or overcasting. Press open.

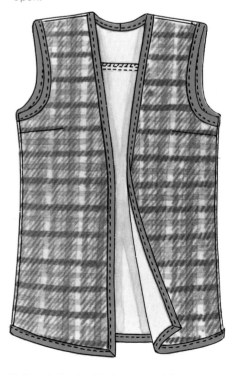

7 Attach the braid trim around the armholes and front, lower and neck edges of the vest, beginning and ending at the center back neck.

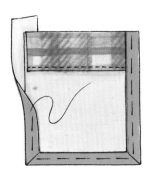

8 Press $\frac{1}{4}$in (6mm) to wrong side at top edge of pocket and finish with a row of machine stitching or overcasting. Press the pocket facing to the wrong side on the foldline. Baste the braid trim to the side and lower edges of the pocket, folding in raw ends at top corners of pocket and mitering corners. Press.

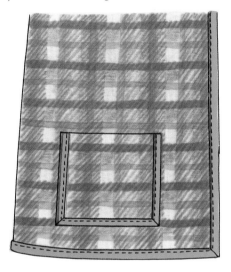

9 Baste the pockets to the front of the vest in the positions marked. Stitch close to the inner edge of the braid to secure the pockets in place.

10 Make two miters and ties as shown on page 72. Sew them to the front of the vest in the positions marked.

Terry Evans

Gary Warren

75

*Working with silk fabric
*Inverted box pleats
*Loose-lining a skirt
*Skirt with inverted box pleats:
adapting the pattern;
directions for making (1)

Working with silk fabric

Silk is a natural fiber which is woven into several different fabrics. Raw silk is coarsely woven and can be treated the same as other medium-weight fabrics, but lightweight fabrics such as crepe de chine, pongee, shantung and silk chiffon need extra care when being sewn, as they are soft and tend to slip. When working with silk, use pure silk thread or a suitable synthetic thread and fine needles. A machine needle size 17 or 18 is usually used on fine fabrics like silk.

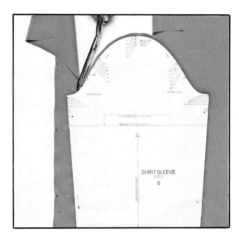

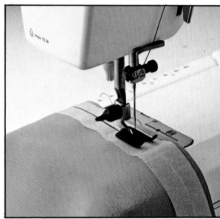

1 When cutting out silk fabric, if possible pin it to a sheet, as this will help keep the silk from moving as you cut. Place the pins within the seam allowance so they don't mark the fabric. If the fabric tends to ravel badly, allow an extra $\frac{1}{4}$in (6mm) on the seam allowance. Cut out the pattern pieces carefully, avoiding cutting into the sheet.

2 To keep seams from slipping, place tissue paper above and below the fabric before sewing through all layers.

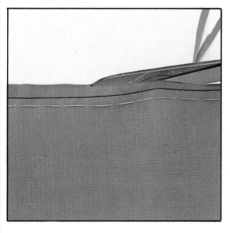

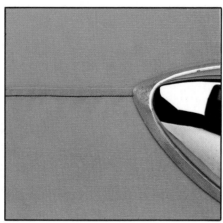

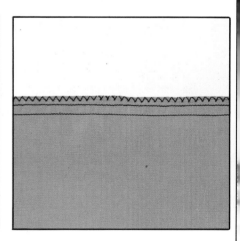

3 The seam most often used on silk fabrics is a French seam, as this prevents the raw edges from raveling and from showing through on sheer fabrics. Place wrong sides of the two pieces together, then pin and baste along seamline. Sew seam approximately $\frac{1}{4}$in (6mm) outside seamline. Tear away tissue paper, trim seam allowance to $\frac{1}{8}$in (3mm) and press seam open.

4 Bring the right sides of the fabric together with the stitching on the fold. Baste and sew on the seamline to enclose the raw edges. Press the seam to one side.

5 An alternative seam suitable for silk is the double-stitched seam. Make the first line of stitches in the normal way on the seamline with the right sides of the fabric together. Make a second row of stitches $\frac{1}{4}$in (6mm) outside the seamline. Trim the remaining seam allowance to $\frac{3}{8}$in (1cm) and overcast the raw edge by hand or machine.

Inverted box pleats

An inverted box pleat is formed by a pair of single pleats facing each other and just meeting with the fabric beneath them forming the inverted box pleat.

When used on a crisp fabric, this type of pleat looks better pressed, while box pleats in soft fabrics—such as silk—are better left unpressed.

Inverted box pleats are usually about 2-4in (5-10cm) wide, the distance between them varying with the pattern. When several pleats are used in one section of a garment they can be made quite narrow, in which case the folds of fabric on the wrong side will not overlap. Whether or not you choose to sew these pleats down depends on the style of the garment. They can be left unstitched to fall from a waistband, or topstitched in place down to the release point, which is usually the fullest part of the hip; or stitched from the wrong side of the garment so that no stitches are visible on the right side of the pleat.

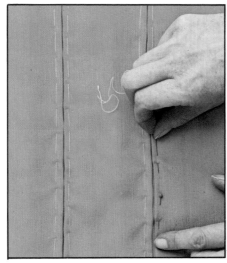

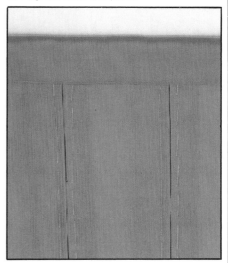

1 Transfer the pleat lines from the pattern to the fabric with lines of basting. Place the fabric on a flat surface with the right side facing up. Fold each pleat in place matching the basting line for the fold (the outside line in each set of pleats) to the center line.

2 Pin each pleat into position and baste $\frac{1}{4}$in (6mm) from fold through all thicknesses, from hem of the garment to top. This will prevent the pleats from stretching if they are off grain. If you are making pressed pleats, press them at this stage.

3 If the pleats are to be left unstitched to fall from a waistband, leave the basting in the pleats until you have attached the waistband as shown in Volume 2, page 50.

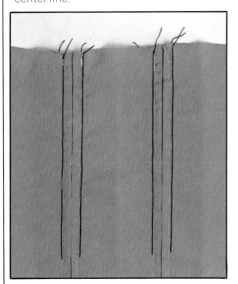

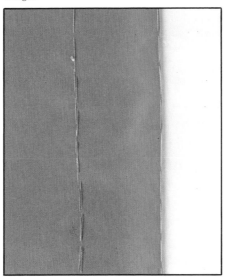

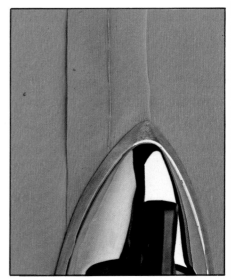

4 For topstitched pleats, measure down each pleat foldline from the waistline to the release point. Mark this point with a pin. Topstitch the pleat (shown here in a contrasting color) from the hip to the waist, $\frac{1}{4}$in (6mm) from the fold. Anchor the thread ends on the wrong side and press again (for pressed pleats only).

5 To stitch the pleats in place from the wrong side of the fabric, fold the fabric with right sides together, matching the outside foldlines of each pleat. Baste from the release point to the waistline, on the basting line marking the pleat.

6 Sew along the pleat from the release point to the waistline along the line of basting. Remove the basting and press the box pleat flat from the wrong side. Fold, baste and sew the other pleats the same way.

Loose-lining a skirt

Lining a skirt will not only improve its wear but will also help it to retain its shape, add body to the main fabric and provide a neat, finished look to the inside of the garment. Choose a lining suitable in weight and texture for the fabric being used. For silk fabrics, use a lightweight lining such as silk organza, china silk or silk-like polyester. Heavy fabrics need a more durable lining such as taffeta, silk surah or medium-weight polyester crepe.

The lining for a skirt may be cut from the same pattern pieces as the skirt itself, or, if the skirt is pleated, a separate pattern may be given.

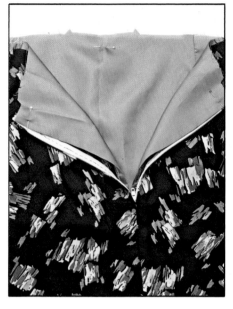

1 Assemble the skirt and lining separately, then join them at the waist seam.
Insert the lining inside the skirt, matching waistlines, side seams, center fronts and center backs. Normally the lining is placed inside the skirt with the wrong sides together. On sheer fabrics, however, the right side of the lining is placed against the wrong side of the skirt, to prevent the lining seams from showing through.

2 If French seams have been used, clip into the seam on the lining almost to the stitches at the bottom of the zipper opening. Overcast the top of the French seam and the raw edge of the seam allowance of the zipper opening.

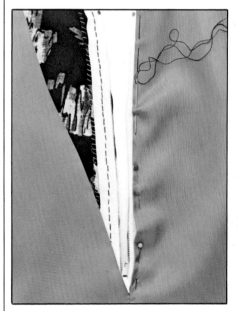

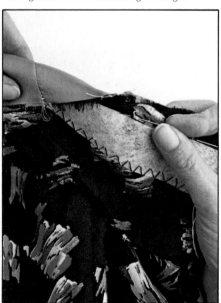

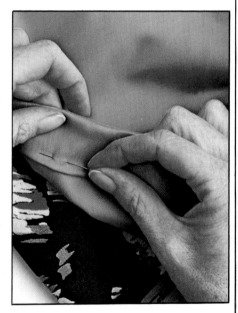

3 Fold in the seam allowances of the lining on both sides of the zipper and baste them in place. Slip stitch the folded edges to the zipper tape. Press.

4 Baste the lining and skirt waist edges together. Treating the two fabrics as one, attach the waistband to the skirt in the regular way as shown in Volume 2, page 50.

5 Try on the skirt and mark the hemline. Turn up the skirt hem. Trim away $\frac{5}{8}$in (1.5cm) from the raw edge of the lining. Fold the original hem allowance to the wrong side on the lining, so that the lining will be $\frac{5}{8}$in (1.5cm) shorter than the skirt when finished. Fold in the raw edge of the hem allowance and stitch it to the lining. Press folded edge of hem only.

Softly suited

This beautiful tunic and skirt are ideal for those occasions when you want to look really elegant. They look especially stunning made from a luxurious silk fabric. Here we give directions for making the skirt; directions for making the tunic appear in Volume 8, page 54.

Adapting the pattern

The skirt is made by adapting the pattern for the A-line skirt from the Stitch by Stitch Pattern Pack, available in sizes 10-20 which correspond to sizes 8-18 in ready-made clothes.

Materials

Sheets of tracing paper 33½x21½in (85x55cm)

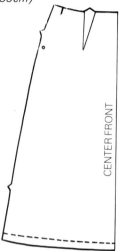

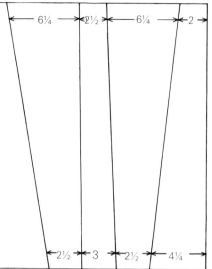

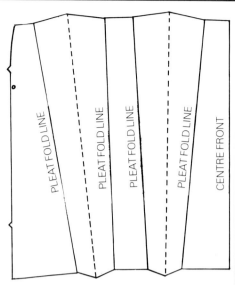

1 Trim 1⅝in (4cm) from hem allowance. To remove waist dart from skirt front, measure the width of the dart at the waist edge. Mark a point at the waistline that distance in from side edge of skirt.

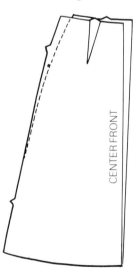

Lay the front pattern over the back pattern, matching the point you have marked at the waist to the side edge of the back and matching the two lower corners together. Trace the hip curve to reshape the front pattern. If you do not want to use the A-line skirt pattern again, trim off the pattern on the new cutting line. If you wish to retain the complete pattern, draw the line thickly so that it can be easily traced in the next steps.

2 On a sheet of paper 4in (10cm) longer than skirt, trace center front line and first 2in (5cm) of waistline and first 4¼in (10.5cm) of hemline. Connect these two points for first pleat line. Mark a point 6¼in (16cm) from new line at waist edge and a point 2½in (6.5cm) from pleat line at hem edge. Join the points to form the second pleat line. Mark the center of the pleat between the two lines just drawn (shown top right).

Measure in a further 2½in (6.5cm) at waistline and 3in (7.5cm) at hemline and join the two points for first line of second pleat. Measure 6¼in (16cm) from this line at waist edge and 2½in (6.5cm) at hem edge and join second line for this pleat. Draw the center line between the two pleat lines just drawn.

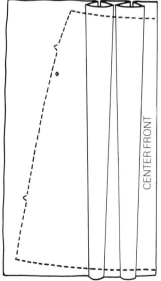

3 Fold the pleats into position and pin in place. Lay the pleated pattern over the re-drawn skirt front, with pleated waist edge overlapping by 2in (5cm) at center front. Re-draw skirt front at waistline, side and hem edges.

4 Cut around the new cutting lines on the pleated section before unpinning the pleats to form the complete hemline and waistline.

5 The skirt back is adapted simply by trimming away 1⅝in (4cm) from hem allowance on lower edge.

6 For the lining use the unaltered skirt back and front, with waist darts.

Directions for making (1)

Suggested fabrics

Silk crepe de chine, pongee, shantung, or other soft fabrics such as Viyella® or crepe.

Materials

44, 45 or 54in (112, 115 or 140cm)-wide fabric with or without nap:
  For all sizes: 2¼yd (2m)
36in (90cm)-wide lining fabric:
  Sizes 10 and 12: 2⅛yd (1.9m)
  Sizes 14, 16, 18 and 20: 2⅜yd (2.1m)
45 or 54in (115 or 140cm)-wide lining fabric:
  Sizes 10, 12, 14, 16 and 18: 2⅛yd (1.9m)
  Size 20: 2¼yd (2m)
36in (90cm)-wide interfacing:
  Sizes 10, 12, 14, 16: 6in (15cm)
  Sizes 18 and 20: 10in (25cm)
Matching thread, 7in (18cm) skirt zipper, skirt hook and eye

Key to adjusted pattern pieces

1 Skirt front	Cut 1 on fold
2 Skirt back	Cut 1 on fold
3 Waistband	Cut 1
Interfacing	use piece 3

1 After the pattern pieces for the skirt front and back as shown here.
2 Prepare the main fabric and pin on the pattern pieces following the layout.
Cut out the pieces and transfer the pattern markings to the fabric.

Tony Boase

3 Prepare the lining fabric and pin on the pieces for the lining front and back following the correct layout for the fabric width you are using. Cut out the pattern pieces from the lining fabric and transfer all pattern markings to the fabric.

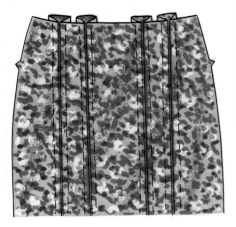

4 Fold and baste the pleats into place on the skirt front as shown on page 77. Do not press.

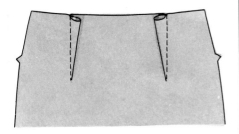

5 Fold, baste and sew the waist darts in the skirt back. Press the darts toward the center back.

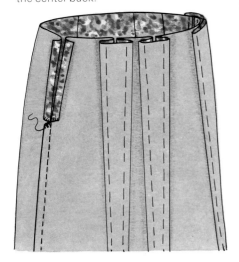

6 Baste and sew the side seams of the skirt using French seams (see page 76). Leave the left side seam open above the dot for the zipper.
7 Clip into the seam allowance at the base of the zipper opening, almost to the stitching line, and press the seam toward the back. Finish the raw edges of the clip by overcasting.

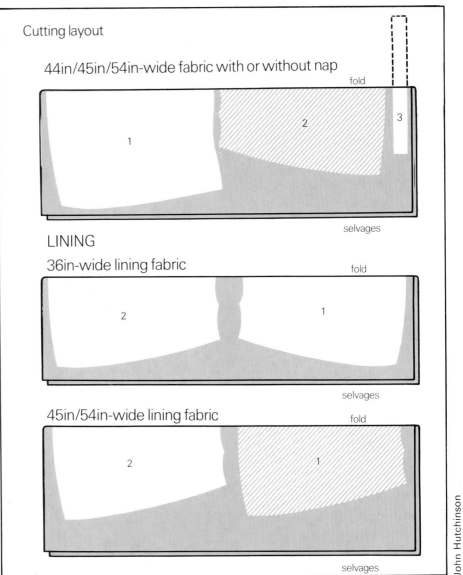

Cutting layout

44in/45in/54in-wide fabric with or without nap

fold

1   2   3

selvages

LINING

36in-wide lining fabric

fold

2   1

selvages

45in/54in-wide lining fabric

fold

2   1

selvages

John Hutchinson

8 Baste and sew the waist darts in the lining front and back and press them toward the center of the skirt. Baste and sew the side seams using French seams and leaving the opening in left side as before. Clip the seam and finish by overcasting.

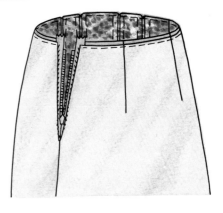

9 If the skirt is being made in silk or a sheer fabric, insert the lining into the skirt with the right side of the lining against the wrong side of the skirt. If the skirt is being made in a heavier fabric, insert the lining into the skirt with wrong sides together.
Baste the skirt and lining together around the waistline. Fold in the seam allowance on the lining at the zipper opening and baste to zipper tape. Slip stitch; press.

10 Interface the waistband to the fold-line only. Baste and sew the waistband to the skirt, right sides together. Fold band in half, right sides together, and join the short ends. Grade the seams and press the waist seam up. Fold the waistband right side out and turn in the raw edge. Slip stitch folded edge to stitching line on wrong side.
Attach the skirt hook and eye to the waistband at the back opening.

11 Try on the skirt and mark the hem. Turn up the hem and baste close to the folded edge. Trim hem allowance to 1 in (2.5 cm) and overcast raw edge by hand. Sew hem in place using invisible hemming stitches. Remove basting stitches and press folded edge of hem only. Turn up lining hem, making it $\frac{5}{8}$ in (1.5 cm) shorter than the skirt. Finish the lining hem in the same way as the skirt hem.

Terry Evans

Tony Boase

Needlework / COURSE 9

Patchwork

Patchwork is a method of creating a large piece of fabric by joining small pieces in a variety of fabrics. From simple beginnings when pioneer women stitched together formless scraps of material into "crazy" quilts, patchwork developed into an art form with geometric shapes joined in elaborate patterns. Modern needleworkers have taken up the art out of admiration for its ingenious effects.

Materials
Use soft, firmly woven fabrics that are colorfast and pre-shrunk if possible for both patches and backing. To join patches, use thread in the same material as the patches and a short, sharp needle, or join by machine.

Straighten all fabrics before use by pulling threads across the top and bottom and cutting along the lines they make. Then pull the material on the bias until the grain line across the fabric is at right angles to the selvages. The fabric should then be pressed.

To make patches, use a cardboard template. Make several of each shape and discard them as they get worn. Templates can be the exact size of the finished patch or they can be the size of the patch plus $\frac{1}{4}$in (5mm) seam allowance with a window the size of the patch in the middle. Patches must be cut in accordance with the grain line of the fabric to avoid stretching. Two opposite sides of squares, rectangles, octagons, hexagons and diamonds should run along the grain. Triangles should have one edge that is on the grain.

Making patches

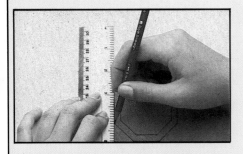 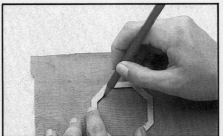 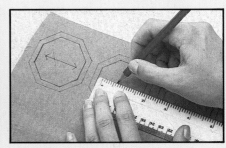

1 Place a solid template on the wrong side of the fabric, carefully aligning one or more edges with the grain line, and trace around it. Remove template. Measure out $\frac{1}{4}$in (5mm) from each edge of shape and draw a larger shape around the first.

2 If you are using a window template, place it on the wrong side of the fabric along the correct grain line. Trace around the outside and the window with a soft pencil.

3 Mark the crosswise grain lightly with a double-pointed arrow on the back of each patch. Cut out all the patches around the outside of the seam allowance. String likes together on a long thread with a knot in the end.

Joining patches

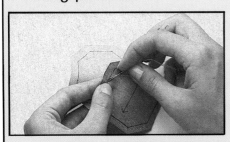 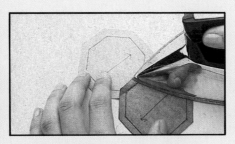 

1 Work from center out. With right sides together and grain lines matching, pin and baste two patches together along seam lines. Machine stitch or hand sew with running stitch or back stitch.

2 Make sure corners where several pieces come together meet exactly. Clip corners as necessary to eliminate bulk. Press seams to one side for added strength.

3 Continue adding pieces until you have completed a block or strip depending on the design. When all segments are completed, assemble them and add borders.

Patchwork art

Stitch a work of art to hang anywhere in your home. Use different materials for different effects or create your own design.

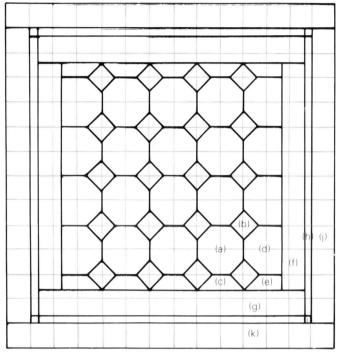

John Hutchinson

1 square = 1 in square

Finished size
14 × 14in (35.5 × 35.5cm) (excluding loops).

Materials
- *Large sheet of graph paper*
- *Colored pencils or crayons*
- *Cardboard*
- *Pencil*
- *Ruler*
- *1 yd (1m) solid color cotton fabric for outer borders, 15 patches, backing and loops.*
- *½yd (.5m) each of two other solid color fabrics for inner borders and patches*
- *½yd (.5m) of printed fabric for middle border and patches*
- *Scrap of contrasting color for corner squares*
- *Matching thread*
- *14in (35.5cm) long wooden dowel ⅜in (1cm) thick*

To make
1 Draw design full size on graph paper.
2 Decide on the fabrics and colors and mark or color your diagram.
3 Trace each patch shape (A–K) on your diagram and transfer to cardboard, leaving at least ½in (1.3cm) between shapes. Measure out ¼in (5mm) from each edge of each shape and draw another larger outline around each shape.
4 Cut out each shape along the outer outline. Then cut out along the inner line. Check the window against your design to be sure it is accurate. You may mark sides of template to be placed along cross grain of fabric.
5 Straighten the grain of each fabric and press to remove all wrinkles.
6 Lay fabrics one at a time face down on a flat surface and place the appropriate templates on them with one or more edges along grain. Trace around the outer edge and inner window with a sharp pencil. Repeat as many times as necessary. You should do 12 A shapes, 20 B shapes, 6 C shapes, 8 D shapes, 4 E shapes, 2 F shapes, 2 G shapes, 4 H shapes, 4 I shapes, 2 J shapes and 2 K shapes.
7 Mark grain on drawn shapes and then cut out and string likes together. Starting with center strips of A's, B's, and C's, sew the pieces together. Clip corners and press seams to one side as you work. Add the remaining A's, B's, C's, D's and E's to complete the center.
8 Now add the borders in the following order: F's, G's, H's, I's, J's and K's.
9 Press the whole panel carefully.
10 Cut a strip of backing fabric 3in (7.5cm) wide and 14in (35.5cm) long and fold in half along its length right sides together. Machine stitch down its length ½in (1.3cm) from edges to form a tube. Turn right side out and press. Cut into 7 2in (5cm-long) segments.
11 Cut out the backing the same size as the patchwork panel.
12 Along top edge of the backing on the right side, mark points ¾in (2cm) in from side edges with tailor's chalk, pencil or pins. From these points, mark points at 1in (2.5cm) intervals all along this edge. Fold loop segments in half with raw edges matching. Place first loop on top of backing between first two marks with raw edges of loop matching raw edge of backing, and pin. Place the other loops 1in (2.5cm) apart along the edge of the backing. Baste securely ¼in (5mm) from edges.
13 Place patchwork top and backing right sides together, loops to the inside; pin and baste ¼in (5mm) from edges. With patchwork side up, sew, starting with seam at bottom edge approximately 4in (10cm) in from side seam and going all around to the bottom edge, leaving a gap of about 6in (15cm).
14 Trim corners and turn work right side out through opening in bottom seam. Hand sew with tiny stitches. Press.
15 Insert dowel through loops.

Needlework / COURSE 10

* Embroidery on clothing
* Cross-stitch designs
* Charting a motif
* Cross-stitch over canvas
* Cross-stitched blouse

Embroidery on clothing

Embroidery is an excellent way to add your own distinctive touch to a garment. Monograms are perhaps the most common form of embroidery on clothing, but the range of suitable styles and designs is virtually limitless.

Before you embroider a piece of clothing you should give careful thought to the positioning of the work. It should look like an integral part of the garment's design, not something stuck on in an arbitrary way. Use the embroidery to highlight some feature of the garment, such as a yoke, a cuff or a patch pocket. If, however, the garment already has plenty of detail in its construction, adding embroidery may produce a fussy look. For the same reason, embroidery is usually confined to solid-color fabrics. Exceptions are fine-checked gingham, which lends itself to cross-stitch, and some fine stripes. Also, you can use embroidery to emphasize the pattern of a floral print, for example, to make it literally "stand out" on chosen parts of the garment.

In some cases the embroidery is worked after the garment is completed—for example, if it covers a seam. More often it is worked on the pattern pieces before assembling. If the stitches can be worked in the hand, you can cut out the pieces as usual and then work the embroidery.

If, however, you need to use a frame, you must use a different method. After pinning on the pattern, draw or baste around the pieces to be embroidered, right on the cutting line. Remove the pattern. Lay the frame over the area to be embroidered and see if there is enough excess fabric outside the cutting line to fill the frame. If so, cut around the piece, allowing the necessary margin. If the cutting layout does not permit this, remove the adjacent pattern piece(s) and work the embroidery on the uncut fabric. Then cut out the pattern and proceed as usual.

Cross-stitch designs

Cross-stitch is well suited to clothing— particularly to informal clothes. For centuries it has been used on peasant costume in central Europe and Asia, often in highly intricate patterns. Its angular shape gives it a crisp look, enhanced by the use of bright, clear colors on white fabric, but it can easily be used for graceful curved shapes and lines. By using two shades of the same

Peter Pugh-Cook

color in a motif you can even suggest depth.

Suitable designs are easy to find. Your library probably has books containing designs already charted for cross-stitch or needlepoint. Or you could use a stencil design or perhaps a photograph or drawing of a plant, animal or object, provided it has a clear shape that will make it easily recognizable when it has been stitched.

Charting a motif

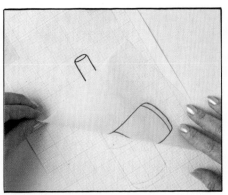

Fred Mancini

1 Trace the outline of the motif, simplifying or omitting details; what you want is a good, strong shape. Then turn the tracing over and go over the lines on the wrong side with a dark, soft pencil.

2 Place the tracing right side up on a piece of graph paper. Make sure that the grid lines run exactly as you want the stitches to run in the finished work; tape the tracing in place. Now go over the motif outlines firmly with a ball point pen to transfer the pencil marks to the graph paper.

3 Color the squares to represent the stitches. Where the outline goes through a square, color it if half or more of the square lies inside the motif; otherwise leave it blank. Use the original drawing or photograph as a guide to shading, if desired.

Cross-stitch over canvas

Cross-stitch can be worked on finely woven fabric with the help of needle-point canvas. The canvas must be the kind that can be raveled—that is, the interlock type—but it can be either Penelope (double thread) or mono canvas. In our sample we have used No. 18 mono canvas. The stitches are worked over the threads of the canvas (in this case over 3 horizontal and 3 vertical threads), which are later removed.

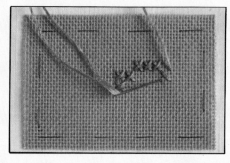

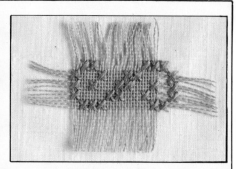

1 Lay the piece of canvas (slightly larger than the motif) on top of the fabric. Make sure the fabric is smooth and straight and that the canvas threads run correctly for the motif. Baste the canvas in place around the edges.
Work the embroidery over the canvas. Make sure that top stitches all slant in same direction.

2 When the stitching is complete, remove the basting. Saturate a towel with hand-hot water and place it on top of the work for a few minutes to moisten the canvas thoroughly. Then gently ease out the canvas threads. If the embroidered area is large, cut the canvas between motifs to make the threads easier to remove.

Traditional charm

The appeal of cross-stitch is evident in this charming blouse. We've used the pattern from Sewing course 5 (see Volume 1, page 60) and made it in a cool linen-cotton blend with a shantung-type weave.

Materials

> Blouse pattern given in Sewing course 5
> Blouse fabric and notions (see page 84)-omit cuff interfacing unless fabric is very soft
> $\frac{3}{8}$yd (.3m) of No. 18 mono canvas, 28in (70cm) wide
> 4 skeins of stranded embroidery floss in dark blue
> 4 skeins of stranded embroidery floss in light blue
> No. 22 tapestry needle

To make

1 Cut out and prepare the pattern pieces following the appropriate layout in Volume 1, page 61 and steps 1-3 in Volume 1, page 60.
2 Finish the raw edges (except on bias strips) with zig-zag stitch or hand-overcasting.
3 Cut two pieces of canvas 1½in (4cm) less than width of cuff and 1¼in (3.5cm) deep. Mark the center of the canvas (widthwise) with hard pencil or indelible pen.
4 Mark the foldline and vertical center of the cuff piece with basting.
5 Baste each piece of canvas to the right side of each cuff (see Step 1 above), matching one of the long sides of the canvas with the fold line of the cuff and

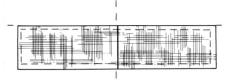

the center mark of the canvas with the center of the cuff.

6 Using light blue embroidery floss, work the cuff design. (Use six strands for all the embroidery.) Begin at the center line, 14 holes down from the fold line and work as instructed in Needlework course 5, Volume 3, page 71. Work the first stitch of the scroll motif (circled on the chart), then continue to the left; then work from center to right.

7 Apply the sleeve facing to each sleeve as shown in Volume 1, page 58.

8 Cut two pieces of canvas, each $3\frac{1}{2} \times 16\frac{1}{2}$in ($9 \times 42$cm). Baste each piece of canvas to the right side of a sleeve, aligning the canvas threads with the grain of the

fabric. For the right sleeve place the canvas to the right of the sleeve opening, as shown, with the excess canvas overlapping the right-hand edge; on the left sleeve the placement is reversed. The lower edge of the canvas should be 2in (5cm) up from the cutting edge of the sleeve. Baste the canvas up to about $1\frac{1}{2}$in (4cm) from the side edge of the sleeve.

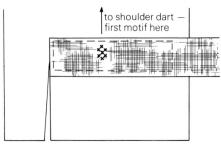

9 Using a straightedge, find the point on the canvas that lines up with the shoulder

dart. Begin the embroidery at this point with the larger motif, placing it in line with the dart and with its base $\frac{5}{8}$in (1.5cm) higher than the top of the sleeve opening. Work the dark blue parts first, then fill in the light blue areas.

10 Work the embroidery up to the basting lines at the sleeve opening and side sleeve edge.

11 Baste and sew the sleeve seam and press it open. Baste the end of the canvas over the seam, matching it at the sleeve opening with the other end of the canvas. Continue the embroidery over the seam and up to the sleeve opening, working a line of cross-stitches to join the motifs on each side of it, as shown on the chart.

12 Cut a piece of canvas $8\frac{1}{2} \times 10$in (21.5×25cm). Mark the center lengthwise by withdrawing a thread.

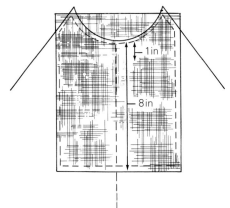

13 Mark the center front of the blouse with a line of basting. Match the center of the canvas with the center of the blouse and baste canvas in place. The lower edge of the canvas should be 8in (20cm) from the center front neck cutting line.

14 From this cutting line measure down 1in (2.5cm) along the withdrawn thread on the canvas. Count 10 canvas holes to the right and begin your first stitch (marked on chart) in this hole. Complete the dark blue part of the pattern, then work the light blue areas.

15 When you have finished all the embroidery, moisten the work and draw out all canvas threads, as shown in step 2, page 86. Press the embroidery on the wrong side.

16 Assemble the blouse as instructed in Volume 1 on pages 61-62 and 66-67, omitting cuf interfacing unless required.

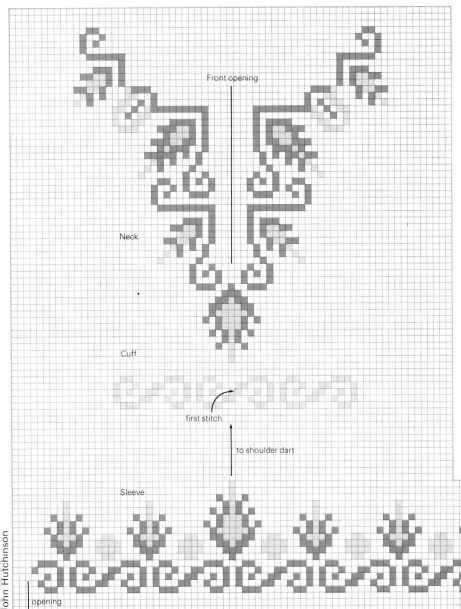

CROCHET

Pretty posies

This loose-fitting cardigan is softly pleated at the front. It is decorated on the front and shoulders with flower motifs.

Sizes

To fit 32[34:36:38]in (83[87:92:97]cm) bust.
Length, 21¼in (54cm).
Sleeve seam, 17[17:17½:17½]in (44 [44:45:45]cm).
Note Directions for larger sizes are in brackets []; where there is only one set of figures it applies to all sizes.

Materials

9[9:10:10] x 2oz (50g) balls of a lightweight mohair
Odds and ends of sport yarn for embroidery
Sizes F and H (4.00 and 5.50mm) crochet hooks
1 pair No. 3 (3¼mm) knitting needles
4 buttons

Gauge

10hdc to 3in (7.5cm) using size H (5.50mm) hook.

Back

Using size H (5.50mm) hook make 83 [86:89:92] ch.
Base row 1hdc into 3rd ch from hook, 1 hdc into each ch to end. Turn. 82[85: 88:91] sts.
Next row (eyelet-hole row) 2 ch to count as first hdc, 1 hdc into each of next 2 hdc, *1ch, skip 1 hdc, 1hdc into each of next 2hdc, rep from * ending with 1hdc in top of turning ch. Turn.
Next row 2ch, 1hdc into each hdc and 1ch sp to end. Turn.
Patt row 2ch, 1hdc into each hdc to end. Turn.
Cont in patt until work measures 10½in (27cm).
Shape armholes
Next row Sl st into 4th hdc, 2ch, 1hdc into next hdc, patt to last 3hdc, turn.
Cont in patt, dec 1 hdc (by skipping first and last hdc of row) at each end of every row until 50[53:56:59] sts rem. Patt 7 rows without shaping.
Shape shoulders
Next row Sl st over first 5[5:6:7] hdc, 1sc into each of next 5hdc, patt to last 10[10:11:12] hdc, 1sc into each of next 5hdc. Fasten off.
Waistband
Using No. 3 (3¼mm) needles and with RS facing, pick up and K 82[85:88:91] sts along other side of base row. Work 19 rows K1, P1 ribbing, beg alternate rows P1 for 2nd and 4th sizes. Bind off in ribbing.

Right front

Using size H (5.50mm) hook make 59 [61:63:64]ch. Work base row as for back. 58[60:62:63] sts.
Next row (eyelet-hole row) 2ch, 1hdc into each of next 2hdc, *1ch, skip 1hdc, 1hdc into each of next 2hdc, rep from * to last 1[0:2:0] hdc, 1 hdc into each of last 1[0:2:0] hdc. Turn.
Next row 2ch, 1hdc into each hdc and 1ch sp to end. Turn.
Next row (1st buttonhole row) Patt to last 4hdc, 1ch, skip 1hdc, 1hdc into each of last 3hdc. Turn.
Next row Patt to end, working 1hdc into 1ch sp over buttonhole. Turn.
Patt 3 more rows.
Next row (2nd buttonhole row) 2ch, 1hdc into each of next 2hdc, 1ch, skip 1hdc, 1hdc into each hdc to end. Turn.
Next row Patt to end, working 1hdc into 1ch sp over buttonhole. Turn. Patt 3 rows, then rep first buttonhole row again.
Next row Patt to end, working 1hdc into 1ch sp over buttonhole. Turn.
Shape front edge
Dec 1hdc at front edge on next and every other row until work measures 10½in (27cm), ending at side edge.
Shape armhole
Next row Sl st into 4th hdc, 2ch, 1hdc into next hdc, patt to last hdc, turn. Dec 1hdc at armhole edge on every row, **at the same time** cont to dec at front edge as before until 10[10:11:11]hdc have been decreased at front edge. Keeping front edge straight, cont to dec at armhole edge until 32[34:35:36] sts rem. Fasten off.
Waistband
Using No. 3 (3¼mm) needles and with RS facing, pick up and K 48[50:52:54] sts along other side of base row. Work 9 rows K1, P1 ribbing.
Next row (buttonhole row) Rib to last 4 sts, bind off 2 sts, rib 2.
Next row Rib to end, casting on 2 sts

over those bound off in last row. Rib another 8 rows. Bind off in ribbing.

Left front

Work as for right front, omitting buttonholes.

Right yoke

Using size H (5.50mm) hook make 16 [16:17:18]ch. Work base row as for back. 15[15:16:17]hdc. Patt 7 rows.
Shape shoulder
Next row 2ch, 1hdc into each of next 4 hdc, 1 sc into each of next 5 hdc. Fasten off.

Left yoke

Work as for right yoke to shoulder.
Shape shoulder
Next row Sl st over first 5[5:6:7]hdc, 1sc into each of next 5hdc, 1hdc into each of next 5hdc. Fasten off.

Sleeves

Using size H (5.50mm) hook make 57ch. Work base row as for back. 56 sts. Cont in patt until work measures 14½[14½: 15:15]in (37[37:38:38]cm) from beg.
Shape top
Work as for back armhole shaping until 24 hdc rem. Fasten off.
Cuffs
Using No. 3 (3¼mm) needles and with RS facing, pick up and K 48 sts along other side of base row. Work 19 rows K1, P1 ribbing. Bind off in ribbing.

To finish

Using sport yarn, embroider flower motif on left front and 4 small flowers on each yoke. Gather top part of fronts to fit along lower edge of yokes, then sew in position. Join shoulder seams, join side and sleeve seams. Set in sleeves.

Edging Using size F (4.00mm) hook and with RS facing, work a row of sc up

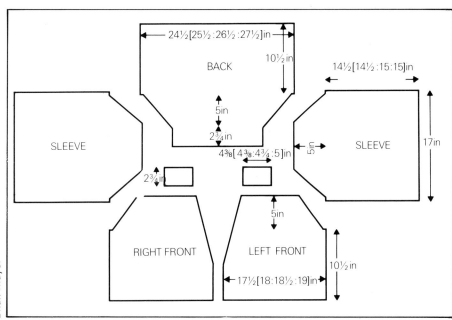

right front edge, around neck edge and down left front edge. Turn and work a 2nd row. Fasten off.

Sew on buttons. Make a twisted cord, using 5 strands of yarn each 5yd (4.5m) long. Thread cord through eyelet holes above waistband.

Technique tip

Stitches used in flower motifs

Stem stitch

Using yarn double, work from left to right, taking small stitches. The yarn always re-emerges on the left side of the previous stitch.

Satin stitch

Using yarn double, work straight stitches close together across the shape as shown in the drawing above.

Daisy stitch

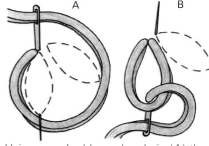

Using yarn double work a chain (A) then fasten loop at outer edge with a small stitch (B). For the large flower work another round of petals outside the first.

French knots

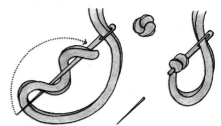

Bring the yarn through fabric from back to front, hold the yarn with the left thumb and wind the yarn twice around the needle. Still holding the yarn, twist the needle back to the starting point and insert it close to where the yarn first emerged (see arrow). This completes first French knot. Then bring needle through to front again at position for next knot. Continue in the same way.

CROCHET

Sitting pretty

This pretty outfit, with a quilt and pillow to match, is quick and easy to make. The sweater has stripes of color and a patterned band across it, with a button closure at the neck. The pants are elasticized so that they can be slipped on and off easily. The quilt is made of individually stuffed squares of crochet.

Stuart Macleod

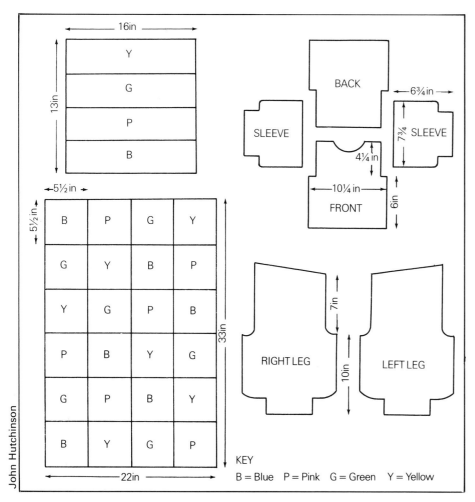

16in

13in

| Y |
| G |
| P |
| B |

5½in

5½in

B	P	G	Y
G	Y	B	P
Y	G	P	B
P	B	Y	G
G	P	B	Y
B	Y	G	P

33in

22in

John Hutchinson

BACK

SLEEVE

SLEEVE

6¾in

7¾in

4¼in

10¼in

FRONT

6in

RIGHT LEG

LEFT LEG

7in

10in

KEY

B = Blue   P = Pink   G = Green   Y = Yellow

To finish

Cut 24 pieces of batting 5in (12cm) × 15in (38cm). Fold in three and insert one piece in each square. Join rem side of each square. Sew squares tog in color order shown in diagram.

Pillow

Using size C (3.00mm) hook and blue make 89ch. Work base row and patt row as for quilt. 88sts. Cont in patt until work measures 3¼in (8cm) from beg. Cut off blue. Join in pink and work a further 3¼in (8cm). Cut off pink. Join in green and work a further 3¼in (8cm). Cut off green. Join in yellow and work a further 6¼in (16cm). Cut off yellow. Join in green and work a further 3¼in (8cm). Cut off green. Join in pink and work a further 3¼in (8cm). Fasten off pink. Join in blue. Work a further 3¼in (8cm). Fasten off.

To finish

Cut a piece of batting 15in (38cm) × 36in (90cm). Fold in three. Sew side seams of pillow. Put batting in pillow. Join rem seam.

Sizes

Quilt 33×22in (84×56cm).
Pillow 13×16in (32×40cm).
Sweater To fit 16-17in (42-44cm) chest.
Length, 10¼in (26cm).
Sleeve, 5½in (14cm).
Pants Inside leg seam, 10in (25cm).

Materials

Sport yarn
Quilt *6oz (150g) in each of pink, yellow, blue and green*
Pillow *2oz (50g) in each of pink, yellow, blue and green*
Sweater *2oz (50g) in each of pink, yellow, blue and green*
1 button
Pants *6oz (150g) in yellow*
Elastic to fit waist
Size C (3.00mm) crochet hook
4½yd (4m) of lightweight batting

Gauge

22hdc and 14 rows to 4in (10cm) worked on size C (3.00mm) hook.

Quilt

Using size C (3.00mm) hook make 32ch.
Base row (WS) 1hdc into 3rd ch from hook, 1hdc into each ch to end. Turn. 31 sts.

Patt row 2ch, skip first hdc, 1hdc into each hdc to end, 1hdc into top of 2ch. Turn. Rep patt row until work measures 5½in (14cm). Fasten off. Work another piece the same color, do not fasten off. With wrong sides tog join pieces as foll: working through double thickness work 31sc along 3 sides, leaving enough yarn to join 4th side, fasten off. Rep to make 6 double squares in each color.

Sweater

Back

Using size C (3.00mm) hook and blue make 57ch.
Base row 1sc into 3rd ch from hook, 1sc into each ch to end. Turn. 56 sts.
Work ¾in (2cm) in sc. Cont in patt as for quilt until work measures 3½in (9cm) from beg. Cut off blue. Join in green.
Puff st row 3ch to count as first hdc and ch, *skip next hdc, yo, insert hook into next hdc and draw a loop through, (yo, insert hook into same hdc, yo, draw a loop through) twice, yo and draw through all loops on hook, 1ch, rep from * to end omitting 1ch on last rep and working 1hdc into last st. Cut off green. Join in pink.

Simon Butcher

Next row 2ch to count as first hdc, 1hdc into each st to end. Turn.
Cont in patt until work measures 6in (15cm) from beg.

Shape armholes

Next row Sl st into each of first 8sts, patt to last 7sts, turn. 42sts.
Cont in patt until work measures 6¾in (17cm) from beg. Fasten off pink. Join in green and work puff st row. Join in yellow and cont in patt until work measures 10¼in (26cm) from beg. Fasten off. Mark center 20sts for back neck.

Front

Work as for back until 4 rows less than back to shoulder have been worked.

Shape neck

1st row Patt 13, dec one st (by working 2sts tog), turn. Dec one st at neck edge on the next 3 rows. Fasten off. Skip center 12 sts, attach yarn to next st, complete to match first side.

Neckband

Join right shoulder seam. Using yellow work a row of sc around neck edge. Cut off yellow. Join in green and work puff st row.
Next row 2ch to count as first sc, 1sc into each st to end. Fasten off.

Sleeves

Using size C (3.00mm) hook and blue make 33ch. Work base row as back. 32 sts. Work 2in (5cm) in sc.
Next row 2ch to count as first sc, 1sc into next sc, *2sc into next sc, 1sc into each of next 2sc, rep from * to end. 42 sts. Cut off blue. Join in green and work puff st row. Cut off green. Join in pink and cont in patt until sleeve measures 6¾in (17cm). Cut off pink. Join in green and work puff st row.
Next row 2ch to count as first sc, 1sc in each st to end. Fasten off.

To finish

Catch edges of left shoulder seam together. Set in sleeves, sewing last 1¼in (3cm) of sleeve seam to 7sts left at armhole shaping. Join side and sleeve seams. Sew button to left shoulder using space between dc as buttonhole.

Pants

Right leg Using size C (3.00mm) hook and yellow make 37ch.
Base row 1sc into 2nd ch from hook, 1sc into each ch to end. Turn. 36sts.
Next row 2ch to count as first sc, skip first sc, 1sc into each sc to end, 1sc in top of 2ch. Turn.
Rep this row for 2in (5cm).
Inc row 2ch to count as first hdc, 1hdc into first sc, 2hdc into each sc to end, 2hdc into top of 2ch. Turn. 72sts.
Cont in patt as on quilt until work measures 10in (25cm) from beg.

Crotch shaping

1st row Sl st to 6th hdc, patt to within last 5hdc, turn. Dec 1hdc at each end of next 5 rows. 52sts. Cont straight until work measures 7in (18cm) from beg of crotch shaping.

Shape back

1st row Sl st into each of first 4sts, 1sc into next st, 1hdc into each st to end. Turn.

2nd row Patt to within last 5sts, 1sc into next st, turn.
Rep last 2 rows 3 times, then first row.
Next row Patt across all sts.
Patt a further 5 rows. Fasten off.

Left leg

Work as right leg reversing all shaping.

To finish

Join inside leg seams, crotch seam. Work herringbone casing over waist elastic.

Sweater set

The short-sleeved pullover has narrow stripes in contrasting colors and the cardigan has diamonds on the shoulders.

Sizes
To fit 36[38:40]in (92[97:102]cm) chest.
Pullover Length 24[25:25]in (60[63: 63]cm). Sleeve seam, 5in (13cm).
Cardigan Length, 25½[26:26] in (65[66: 66]cm).
Sleeve seam, 18½[19:19½]in (47[48:50] cm).
Note Directions for larger sizes are in brackets []; where there is only one set of figures it applies to all sizes.

Materials
18oz (500g) of a sport yarn in main shade (A)
4oz (100g) each of contrasting colors (B, C and D)
1 pair each Nos. 2 and 3 (3 and 3¼mm) knitting needles
No. 2 (3mm) circular needle
5 buttons

Gauge
28 sts and 36 rows to 4in (10cm) in stockinette st on No. 3 (3¼mm) needles.

Pullover

Front
Using No. 2 (3mm) needles and A, cast on 133[141:147] sts.
1st row K1, *P1, K1, rep from * to end.
2nd row P1, *K1, P1, rep from * to end.

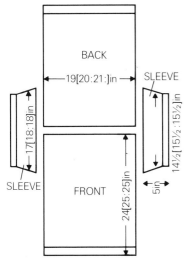

Brian Mavor

Victor Yuan

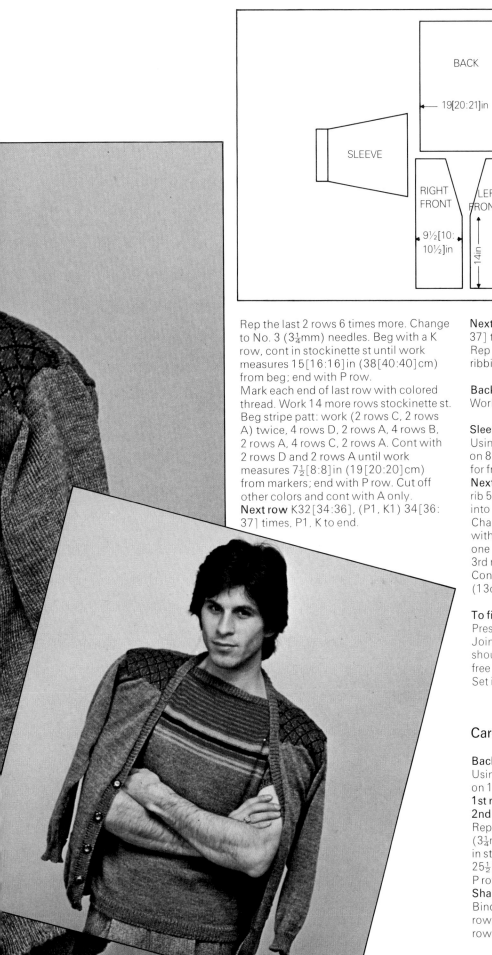

Brian Mayor

Rep the last 2 rows 6 times more. Change to No. 3 (3¼mm) needles. Beg with a K row, cont in stockinette st until work measures 15[16:16]in (38[40:40]cm) from beg; end with P row.

Mark each end of last row with colored thread. Work 14 more rows stockinette st. Beg stripe patt: work (2 rows C, 2 rows A) twice, 4 rows D, 2 rows A, 4 rows B, 2 rows A, 4 rows C, 2 rows A. Cont with 2 rows D and 2 rows A until work measures 7½[8:8]in (19[20:20]cm) from markers; end with P row. Cut off other colors and cont with A only.

Next row K32[34:36], (P1, K1) 34[36:37] times, P1, K to end.

Next row P32[34:36], (K1, P1) 34[36:37] times, K1, P to end.
Rep last 2 rows 4 times more. Bind off, in ribbing over ribbed section.

Back
Work as for front, using A throughout.

Sleeves
Using No. 2 (3mm) needles and A, cast on 89[91:91] sts. Work 9 rows ribbing as for front waistband.
Next row Rib 11, (work twice into next st, rib 5[3:3]) 11[17:17] times, work twice into next st, rib to end. 101[109:109] sts. Change to No. 3 (3¼mm) needles. Beg with a K row, cont in stockinette st, inc one st at each end of 5th and every foll 3rd row until there are 119[127:127] sts. Cont straight until work measures 5in (13cm); end with P row. Bind off loosely.

To finish
Press or block according to yarn used. Join side seams as far as markers. Join shoulder seams, leaving ribbed section free for neck opening. Join sleeve seams. Set in sleeves.

Cardigan

Back
Using No. 2 (3mm) needles and A, cast on 133[141:147] sts.
1st row K1, *P1, K1, rep from * to end.
2nd row P1, *K1, P1, rep from * to end.
Rep last 2 rows 9 times. Change to No. 3 (3¼mm) needles. Beg with a K row, cont in stockinette st until work measures 25½[26:26]in (65[66:66]cm); end with P row.
Shape shoulders
Bind off 22[24:24] sts at beg of next 2 rows and 23[24:25] sts at beg of foll 2 rows. Leave rem sts on holder.

across back and twist them when changing colors to avoid a hole) until work is same as back to shoulder; end at armhole edge.

Shape shoulder
Bind off 22[24:24] sts at beg of next row. Work 1 row. Bind off rem 23[24: 25] sts.

Right front
Work as for left front from ** to **
Divide for pocket
Next row K14 sts, sl next 35 sts onto a holder for pocket, K across 35 sts of pocket lining, K to end. Finish as for left front from *** to end, reversing shaping.

Sleeves
Using No. 2 (3mm) needles and A, cast on 61[63:65] sts. Rib 19 rows as for back waistband.
Next row Rib 3[4:5], *work twice into next st, rib 4, rep from * to last 3[4:5] sts, work twice into next st, rib to end. 73[75:77] sts.
Change to No. 3 (3¼mm) needles. Beg with a K row, cont in stockinette st, inc one st at each end of 5th and every foll 4th[5th:5th] row until there are 119 [127:127] sts. Cont without shaping until work measures 18½[19:19½]in (47[48:50]cm); end with P row. Bind off loosely.

Front band
Join shoulder seams. Using No. 2 (3mm) circular needle, A and with RS facing, beg at lower edge of right front and pick up and K 126 sts up right front to marker, 67[73:73] sts up right side of neck, K across sts on holder, pick up and K 67[73:73] sts down left side to marker and 126 sts down left front. 429[443: 447] sts. Work back and forth in rows.
1st row (WS) P1, *K1, P1, rep from * to end.
2nd row K1, *P1, K1, rep from * to end. Rep last 2 rows once more.
Next row (buttonhole row) Rib 5, (bind off 4, rib 23 — including st used in binding off) 4 times, bind off 4, rib to end.
Next row Rib to end, casting on 4 sts over those bound off in last row. Rib 5 more rows. Bind off loosely in ribbing.

Pocket tops
Using No. 2 (3mm) needles, A and with WS facing, K across 35 sts of pocket top on holder.
1st row (WS) P1, *K1, P1, rep from * to end.
2nd row K1, *P1, K1, rep from * to end. Rep last 2 rows 4 times, then first row again. Bind off loosely in ribbing.

To finish
Do not press. Join side seams to within 8½[9:9]in (22[23:23]cm) of shoulder. Join sleeve seams. Set in sleeves. Sew pocket linings in position on WS and pocket tops on RS. Sew on buttons.

Left front
**Using No. 3 (3¼mm) needles and A, cast on 35 sts for pocket lining. Beg with a K row, work 36 rows stockinette st. Cut off yarn and leave sts on a holder. Using No. 2 (3mm) needles and A, cast on 67[71:73] sts. Rib 20 rows as for back waistband. Change to No. 3 (3¼mm) needles. Beg with a K row, work 36 rows stockinette st. **

Divide for pocket
Next row K18[22:24] sts, sl next 35 sts onto a holder for pocket top, then K across 35 sts of pocket lining, K to end.
***Beg with a P row, cont in stockinette st until work measures 14in (36cm) from beg; end with P row. Mark end of last row with colored thread to denote front (neck) edge.

Shape front edge
Dec one st at front edge on next and every foll 3rd row until 45[48:49] sts rem; end with P row. Beg colorwork patt. Cont in stockinette st, foll chart (strand yarns

The chart:

10										9
8										7
6										5
4										3
P→2										1 ←K

rep 10 sts
1st size
2nd size
3rd size

□ =A   ☒ =B   ⊗ =D

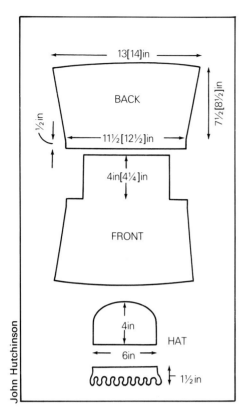

13[14]in

BACK

½in

11½[12½]in

7½[8½]in

4in[4¼]in

FRONT

4in

HAT

6in

1½in

John Hutchinson

Sizes

To fit 16[20]in (41[51]cm) chest.
Length from top of bib, 11½[12¾]in
(29[32]cm).
Note Directions for the larger size are in
brackets []; where there is only one set of
figures it applies to both sizes.

Materials

*4[5] × 1oz (20g) balls of sport yarn
   in main color (A)
1[2] balls of contrasting color (B)
1 pair each Nos. 2 and 3 (3mm and
   3¼mm) knitting needles
Size C (3.00mm) crochet hook
2 small buttons*

Gauge

28 sts to 4in (10cm) in stockinette st
on No. 3 (3¼mm) needles.

Sundress

Back

Using No. 3 (3¼mm) needles and A, cast
on 93[103] sts. Work 4 rows garter st.
Beg with a K row, work 8 rows
stockinette st.
Next row K6, (P1, K9) 8[9] times, P1,
K6. Beg with a P row, work 8 rows
stockinette st, dec one st at each end of
first row. Work 3 rows garter st. Beg patt.
1st row P to end.
2nd row K4, *P3, K7, rep from * ending
with K4.
3rd row P4, *K3, P7, rep from * ending
with P4.
4th row As 2nd.
5th row P to end.
6th row K to end.

7th row K2, *P7, K3, rep from * ending
with K2.
8th row P2, *K7, P3, rep from * ending
with P2.
9th row As 7th.
10th row K to end.
Rep last 10 rows, dec one st at each end
of first and every foll 10th row until
83[91] sts rem. Cont straight until work
measures 7[8]in (17.5[20]cm) from
beg. Change to No. 2 (3mm) needles. **
Next row K1, *P1, K1, rep from * to end.
Next row P1, *K1, P1, rep from * to end.
Rep last 2 rows twice. Cut off A and join
in B. Rib 1 row. Bind off in ribbing.

Front

Work as for back to **.
Next row Rib 13[15], patt 57[61], rib
13[15].
Rep last row 5 times more. Join in B.
Next row Using B, rib 13[15], using A,
patt 57[61], using B, rib 13[15].
Divide for bib
Next row Using B, bind off 13[15] sts,
using A, patt 57[61], using B, bind off
13[15]. Change to No. 3 (3¼mm) needles.
Keeping a garter st border of 2 sts at each
end of every row, cont in patt for
3¾[4]in (9.5[10]cm), dec one st at each

end of 7th and every foll 8th row. Work 3
rows garter st. Bind off.
Pocket
Using No. 3 (3¼mm) needles and A, cast
on 16 sts. Work 4 rows garter st. Keeping
a garter st border of 2 sts at each end of
every row, work 2in (5cm) stockinette st.
Work 4 rows garter st. Bind off.

Straps (make 2)
Using No. 2 (3mm) needles and A, cast
on 70[75] sts. Work 3 rows garter st.
Next row K3, yo, K2 tog, K to end. Work
3 rows garter st. Bind off.

To finish
Press under a dry cloth with a cool iron.
Join side seams.
Edging Using crochet hook, B and with

RS facing, work in sc all around hem.
Join with a sl st into first st.
Next round *3ch, sl st into same st at base
of ch, sl st into each of next 2 sts, rep
from * to end.
Work edging around bib and straps.
Using P sts as a guide, use B to embroider
daisies around hem and on pocket. Sew
pocket to center of bib. Sew on straps,
with buttonholes at back. Sew on
buttons. Press seams.

Bonnet

Crown
Using No. 3 (3¼mm) needles and A cast
on 83 sts. Work 8 rows garter st. Beg with
a K row, work 4 rows stockinette st.
Next row K6, (P1, K9) 7 times, P1, K6.
Work 8 rows stockinette st. Work 9 rows
garter st, dec one st at end of last row.
Shape top
1st row K1, (K2 tog tbl, K16, K2 tog) 4
times, K1. K 5 rows.
7th row K1, (K2 tog tbl, K14, K2 tog) 4
times, K1.
K 3 rows.
11th row K1, (K2 tog tbl, K12, K2 tog)
4 times, K1. K1 row.
13th row K1, (K2 tog tbl, K10, K2 tog) 4
times, K1.
Cont to dec in this way on every alternate
row until row 'K1, (K2 tog tbl, K2 tog) 4
times, K1' has been worked. Cut off yarn,
draw through rem sts and fasten off.

Brim
Using No. 3 (3¼mm) needles and A, cast
on 11 sts.
1st and 2nd rows Sl 1, K10.
3rd row Sl 1, K3, turn.
4th row K4.
5th row Sl 1, K4, turn.
6th row K5.
7th row Sl 1, K5, turn.
8th row K6.
9th row Sl 1, K10.
Work backward from 8th to 3rd row.
** Rep from ** to ** until band fits
loosely all around crown. Bind off.

To finish
Join seam at back of crown. Sew brim to
crown loosely. Using B, work crochet
edging as for dress all around brim.
Embroider daisies around crown.

Stuart Macleod

EXTRA SPECIAL **SEWING**

Something fishy

Based on the time-honored fisherman's smock, this traditional shape is designed to bring comfort to the outdoor life. It can be worn by men or women.

Measurements

Finished chest measurement: 39-42in (100-107cm).
Finished length: 28½in (72cm).
⅝in (1.5cm) seam and hem allowances have been included in the measurement diagram.

Suggested fabrics

Canvas, sailcloth or denim are the most usual materials.
If the fabric is too thick you will find it difficult to stitch through all the thicknesses along the flat felled seams.

Note Flat felled seams, sewn on the right side, have been used for all main seams. At each stage the directions for making show which way the seam should be pressed. Detailed directions for trimming and folding in the seam allowances are not given (see Sewing course 25, Volume 6, page 70). The extra width for the larger size is taken up on the shoulder seam. The armhole and collar measurements remain the same.

Materials

3¾yd (3.4m) of 36in (90cm)-wide or 1⅞yd (1.7m) of 54/60in (140/150cm)-wide fabric
Matching thread
Flexible curve
Tailor's chalk
Yardstick

1 For the front, cut a rectangle of fabric 22 x 29½in (56 x 75cm). Fold the fabric in half lengthwise, pin the edges even and, using tailor's chalk, yardstick and flexible curve, draw the pattern shape on the fabric following the appropriate measurements in the diagram. Keeping the fabric folded, cut out. Remove pins and unfold. Repeat for back section.
2 Before cutting out the sleeves, cut a paper pattern to check that the seamline on the sleeve cap matches the seamline on the armhole. For each sleeve cut a rectangle of fabric 21 x 22½in (53 x 57cm). Following the directions for cutting out front and back, cut out the shaping on the sleeve as shown in the appropriate measurement diagram. Sew tailor's tacks to mark armhole center and baste along foldlines, if cuffs are desired. Cut out pocket and collar pieces following directions on measurement diagram. Mark center of pocket with tailor's tacks.

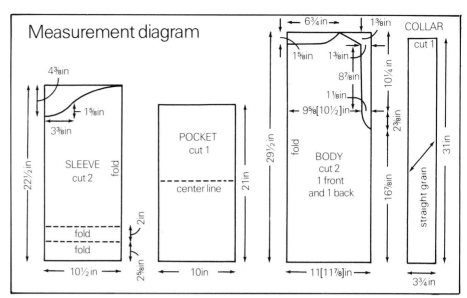

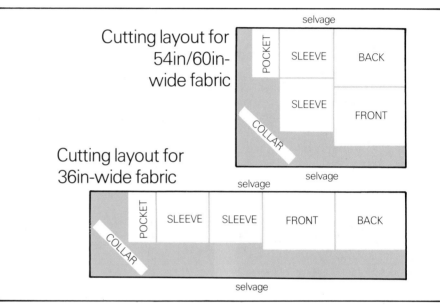

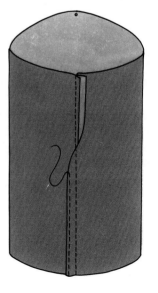

3 With wrong sides together, pin, baste and stitch side and shoulder seams. Trim seam allowance on front section. Fold seam allowances toward the back and topstitch along edge to form a flat felled seam. Press.

4 With wrong sides together, pin, baste and stitch sleeve seams. Fold seam allowances forward and topstitch along edge. Press.

Gary Warren

Terry Evans

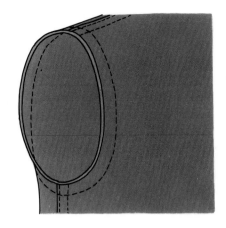

5 Turn sleeve inside out. With body right side out and wrong sides together, insert sleeve in armhole, matching shoulder points and underarm and side seams. Pin, baste and stitch sleeves into armholes. Turn sleeve right side out. Fold seam allowance toward sleeve and topstitch along edge. Press.

6 Turn up sleeve hems, finish and topstitch $\frac{1}{4}$in (6mm) from fold. Repeat for lower hem of smock.

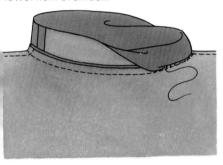

7 Join short ends of collar strip to form a ring and stitch. Press seam. With garment inside out, right sides together, and raw edges even, matching collar seam to one shoulder seam, pin, baste and stitch collar to smock. (Use a plain seam for this.) Press seam upward and trim Turn garment right side out. Turn collar to inside, press along folded edge, turn under seam allowance on free edge, and slip stitch over stitching line around neck.

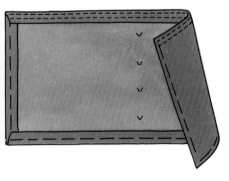

8 Turn under seam allowance all around pocket as shown. Pin, baste and press. Topstitch along top edge only, making first line of stitching close to fold and second line $\frac{1}{4}$in (6mm) lower.

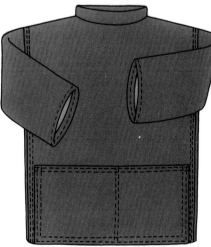

Terry Evans

Gary Warren

9 Position pocket on front of garment, with lower edges even and sides just inside stitching lines on side seams. Topstitch down sides and lower edges as for top edge. Work two parallel lines of topstitching each side of center front line.

If cuffs are required, fold up along marked lines and press.

Old fashioned girl

This delicate camisole and petticoat are too pretty to hide under clothes. Wear them as they are on hot summer days.

Measurements

To fit sizes 10 to 14. The top is 17in (43cm) long at the front and 14in (36cm) long at the back. The finished skirt length is 29in (73cm); adjust at waist before cutting if necessary. A ⅝in (1.5cm) seam allowance and a 1⅝in (4cm) hem allowance are included.

Note Measurements are given for size 10. Measurements for larger sizes are given in brackets[]. If only one figure is given, it applies to all sizes.

Materials

3¼yd (2.9m) 36in (90cm)-wide fabric
4½yd (4m) ruffled eyelet trim,
    ⅝in (1.5cm) wide
1⅛yd (1m) of ¾in (2cm)-wide
    insertion lace
6⅜yd (5.8m) of ¼in (6mm)-wide
    satin ribbon
1½yd (1.3m) of ⅝in (1.5cm)-wide
    bias binding for waist casing
1⅛yd (1m) of ¼in (6mm)-wide
    elastic
14 buttons ⅜in (1cm) in diameter
Matching thread, hook and eye

Suggested fabrics

Lightweight fabrics, such as voile, lawn or eyelet lace.

Camisole

1 Cut out two front pieces and one back piece, following the diagrams and cutting layout on pages 104 and 105. Curve shaping at the top of the front very gently.
2 Mark the waistline 4¾in (12cm) from the lower edge on the front and the back with a line of basting stitches or tailor's chalk. Mark the two fold lines for front facing 1⅛in (3cm) and 2⅜in (6cm) from the raw edge on each side. Mark the center front another ¾in (2cm) in.
3 Mark the lines for the tucks. These are the stitching lines. Fold each tuck, wrong sides together, halfway between the stitching lines. Pin, baste and stitch each tuck in turn. Press tucks outward.

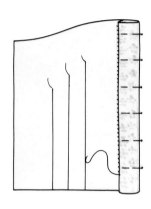

4 Make front facings by turning under a double hem along marked lines on both pieces. Press. Pin in place and slip stitch folded edges in place.

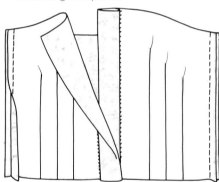

5 Join front sections to back at side seams, right sides together and raw edges matching. Press seams flat.

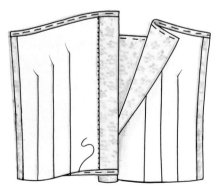

6 Finish upper and lower edges by turning under a ⅜in (1cm) double hem, easing fullness around shaping at top; clip and notch if necessary. Pin and baste in place. Pin and baste eyelet trim around inside of lower edge.

7 Run a line of gathering stitches around top edge. Try on for fit and draw up gathering threads as necessary. (Only a small amount of fullness will need to be taken up.) Fasten gathering threads. Pin and baste eyelet trim in place on inside edge.

8 Topstitch hems and eyelet trim at upper and lower edges. Remove basting and gathering stitches.

9 Mark positions for buttonholes $1\frac{5}{8}$in (4cm) apart down right side of front. Each buttonhole should be $\frac{3}{8}$in (1cm) wide and positioned horizontally. Mark the first one $\frac{3}{8}$in (1cm) from the finished top edge. Mark seven more down the front. Mark two more below the waistline and $\frac{3}{4}$in (2cm) from lower edge. Sew buttonholes. Sew buttons in corresponding positions on the left side.

Tony Boase

Terry Evans

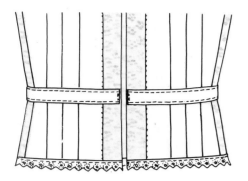

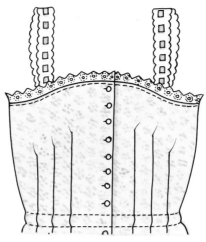

10 At the waistline, pin, baste and stitch bias binding around inside of camisole along upper and lower edges to form a casing. Turn in ends at center front opening. Thread elastic through casing. Fasten one end by sewing securely to front facing. Try on camisole and draw up elastic to fit. Mark required length. Sew second end in place as for first. Attach a hook on right-hand side and eye to left-hand side so that the camisole can be fastened at the waist. Position hook and eye so that they will not show and sew through elastic as well as casing.

11 Cut insertion lace in half. Cut two 19½in (50cm) lengths of ¼in (6mm)-wide ribbon. Thread through lace. Attach straps as shown, finishing ends and adjusting length to fit.
12 Cut six 15¾in (40cm) lengths of ¼in (6mm)-wide ribbon. Tie into bows (see Technique Tip). Sew one bow at top of each tuck on the front of the camisole.

Skirt

1 Cut out front and back sections, waistband and two pockets following the measurement diagrams and cutting layout.
2 Mark tuck stitching lines on skirt and pocket as indicated.
3 Sew side seams of skirt, leaving a 6in (15cm) opening down left-hand side. Press seams open.
4 Sew tucks around skirt as for tucks on top. Press downward. Sew tucks on pockets. Press tucks on left pocket to left and tucks on right pocket to right.

5 Turn under ⅝in (1.5cm) on sides and lower edges of pockets. Press and baste. Turn under a ⅜in (1cm) double hem at

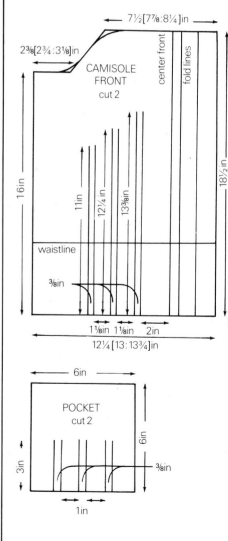

top of pockets. Pin and baste. Cut two pieces of eyelet trim, 5⅛in (13cm) long Turn under ⅜in (1cm) at each end to finish. Run a line of gathering thread through top of pocket. Draw up to fit eyelet trim. Pin edge of eyelet trim to inside of top of pocket. Stitch in place, securing hem at same time.

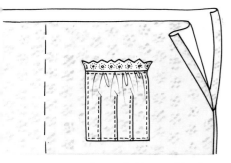

6 Pin pockets to front of skirt, positioning them 6in (15cm) from center front and 6in (15cm) from upper edge so that top of pocket is parallel (insofar as possible) to curved upper edge. Baste in place, then topstitch close to edge.

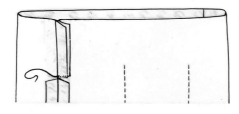

7 Turn under and slip stitch ⅝in (1.5cm)- wide double hems at openings on back and front skirt. Clip into seam allowance of skirt back below opening. Place lower edges of facings together, with front facing outside, and overcast.

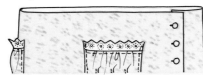

8 Make three ⅜in (1cm) wide buttonholes in the hemmed opening in the front side of the skirt, spacing them 1⅝in (4cm) apart and positioning the lowest 1⅝in (4cm) above the bottom of the opening. Sew three buttons to back to correspond.

9 Cut strip of interfacing for waistband 2in (5cm) deep by 27½[28¾:30⅜]in (70[73:77]cm) long. Baste to wrong side of waistband, matching one long edge of interfacing to center of waistband.

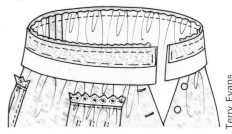

Terry Evans

10 Run two lines of gathering stitches through skirt top and draw up to fit waist. Pin and baste interfaced edge of waistband to top of skirt, right sides together and raw edges even, distributing fullness evenly. Position waistband so that ⅝in (1.5cm) overlaps opening at front and 1¾in (4.5cm) overlaps opening at back, to form the underlap.

11 Turn un-interfaced edge back so that

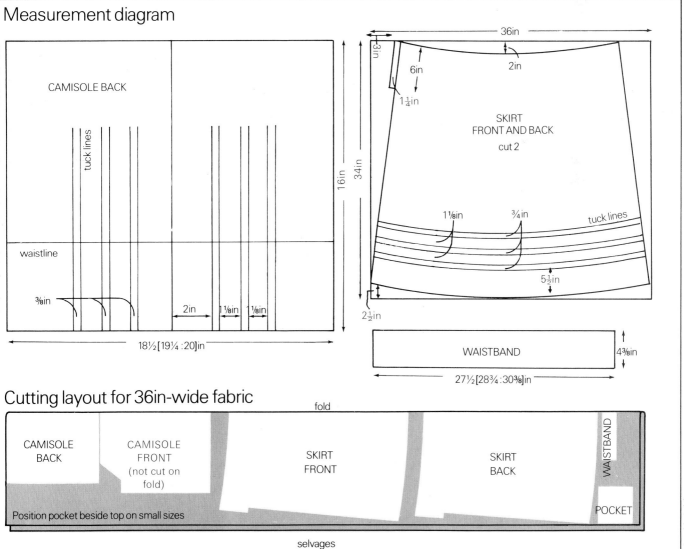

Measurement diagram

CAMISOLE BACK

tuck lines

waistline

⅜in

2in 1⅛in 1⅛in

18½[19¼:20]in

16in

34in

3in

36in

6in

2in

1¼in

SKIRT FRONT AND BACK cut 2

1⅛in   ¾in   tuck lines

5½in

2½in

WAISTBAND

4⅜in

27½[28¾:30⅜]in

Cutting layout for 36in-wide fabric

fold

CAMISOLE BACK

CAMISOLE FRONT (not cut on fold)

SKIRT FRONT

SKIRT BACK

WAISTBAND

POCKET

Position pocket beside top on small sizes

selvages

John Hutchinson

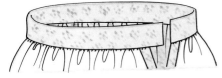

Technique tip

Decorative bows

It is often tricky to tie neat, crisp bows to decorate clothes or packages. This method is very simple.

Sew the bows on carefully so that they cannot come undone. It is advisable to remove the bows before washing, as they are difficult to press when sewn in place. Wash and press the ribbons, tie them up again and sew in place.

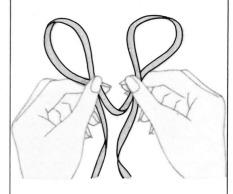

Find the middle of the length of ribbon. Hold the ribbon between thumb and forefinger so that two small loops are formed, one on each side of the center of the ribbon.

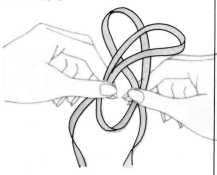

Cross the loop in the left hand over the loop in the right hand.

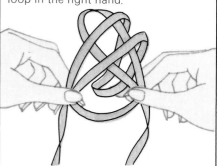

Use the middle finger of your right hand to bend the loop over the loop held in your right hand; then tuck it through the gap between your thumbs. Pull loops tight and adjust tension to form a bow the size you want.

right sides of waistband match. Stitch across ends of waistband and along raw edges of underlap. Clip corners.

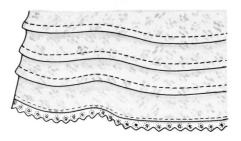

12 Turn waistband right side out. Turn under ⅝in (1.5cm) along remaining raw edge. Slip stitch to skirt, close to line of stitching.

13 Make buttonhole on overlap and sew a ⅜in (1cm) wide button to underlap to match.

14 Try on skirt for fit. Mark hemline 2in (5cm) below lowest tuck. Turn up ⅜in (1cm) around raw edge and stitch. Turn up 1⅝in (4cm) and hem by hand. Sew eyelet trim around inside of hem.

15 Cut six 16in (40cm) pieces of ¼in (6mm)-wide ribbon and tie in bows. Sew to tucks.

Homemaker

Picture the countryside

This attractive fabric collage brings the countryside to life.
It's fun to make too—each part is made individually and then
slotted together to complete the picture.

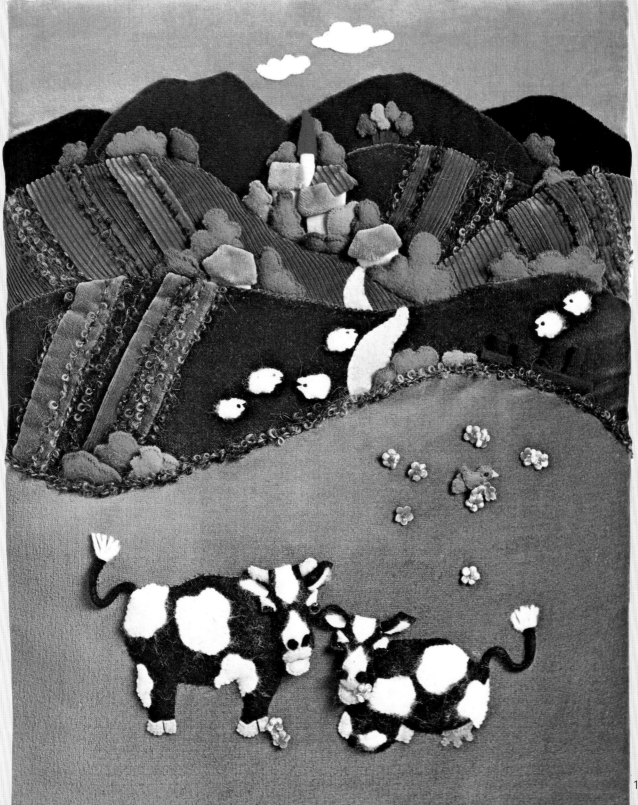

Finished size
18×14in (46×36cm).

Materials
Two pieces of strong backing fabric,
cotton or burlap, one piece 26 x
22in (66 x 56cm) and one piece
19¾ x 15¾in (50 x 40cm)
Remnants of velvet in three shades of
blue, dark green, emerald green and
tan
Scraps of corduroy in tan, brown and
green
Felt in three shades of green, dark
brown, white, red, black, pink,
beige, blue and yellow
One pipe cleaner
Two sets of small glass eyes
Short lengths of bouclé yarn in
green/brown mixture
Small pink fabric flowers
Batting or absorbent cotton for
stuffing
Matching sewing threads
Tracing paper
Dressmaker's carbon paper
Plywood, strong cord and screw
eyes for mounting and hanging

This collage is made up in sections,
following the diagram, in alphabetical
order. The bushes, trees, fields, animals
and flowers are appliquéd to their respec-
tive hills before the hills are stitched
in place.

Cutting out and background (A)
1 Trace all the patterns. Using
dressmaker's carbon paper mark out as
many as indicated of each piece on the
wrong side of the appropriate fabrics.
Choose appropriate colors and fabrics
for each piece: green felt for the trees and
bushes, beige and white felt for the
houses, velvet and corduroy for the roofs,
white felt for the sheep and so on. The
photograph on page 107 gives some
idea of suitable colors.
Cut out each piece and group together.
2 Make patterns for the hill shapes B, D, E,
G, K, I, M and Q. Start by drawing a
rectangle the same size as the finished
picture on tracing paper. Then sketch in
the hill shapes freehand following the
picture as a rough guide. They don't need
to be exactly the same as the original.
You can then trace the individual hill
patterns. When cutting out the hills, allow
½in (1.2cm) for turning under on the top
edges and extend the lower edge by 1¼in
(3cm) to allow for the next layer to
overlap. At the extreme right and left
edges, add 4in (10cm) to extend the
edges of the hills to width of backing.
3 On the larger piece of backing fabric,
mark the finished size of the collage,
centering the rectangle on the fabric.
4 From pale blue velvet cut out a piece
22×8¼in (56×21cm) for the sky (A). Pin
and baste to the backing in position.

Hills (B)

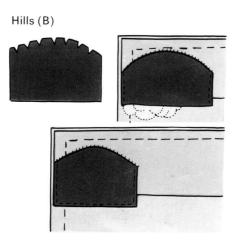

Cut out both hills from dark blue velvet.
Clip around the top curved edge. Turn
top edge to wrong side and baste. Place
both hills in place on backing fabric, over
sky. Baste and slip stitch around top edge
Baste and stitch sides down flat. Insert
some stuffing through base, then baste
and stitch base edges flat.

Bushes (C)

Place together in pairs; baste and overcast
edges together, leaving base edges open.
Fill each bush through base. Place
bushes in position; baste and stitch down
along base edges.

Hills (D and E)
Cut out from medium blue velvet. Make
hills and stitch them in place on backing
fabric, as for hills (B).

Bushes and trees (F)

Make and sew in place, as for bushes
(C). Place treetops together in pairs;
baste and overcast edges together, stuffing
as you work. Group treetops in position
over tree trunks; catch-stitch in place.

Hill (G)

Cut out from emerald green velvet. From
brown corduroy cut two strips, one ¾in
(2cm) wide and one 1in (2.5cm) wide,
for fields. Baste and slip stitch in
place down the hill at an angle. Couch
stitch (see Volume 1, page 125) bouclé
yarn down the edges of the corduroy fields
and down the hill. Complete hill and sew
in place, as for hills (B).

Bushes and houses (H)

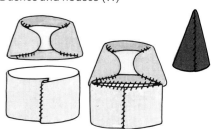

Make bushes as for bushes (C). Turn in
roof edges of houses along broken lines;
baste and slip stitch on wrong side. Turn
in sides of houses along broken lines;
baste and slip stitch on wrong side. Baste
and slip stitch walls to roofs on the wrong
side. Make church as for houses. Position
houses, church and bushes at one end of
hill (G). Baste and sew in place,
stuffing as you work.

Hill (I)
Cut out from tan corduroy, using ribs of
cord to suggest furrows. From brown
corduroy cut two ¾in (2cm)-wide strips
for fields. Baste and sew corduroy and
pieces of bouclé yarn to hill and complete
as for hill (G).

Bushes (J)
Make and stitch in place as bushes (C).

Hill (K)

Cut out from brown corduroy. From tan
corduroy cut out two strips for fields, one
1in (2.5cm) wide and one 1¼in (3.5cm)
wide. Baste and sew corduroy and
pieces of bouclé yarn to hill, as for (G).
Baste and slip stitch path (K) in place
Complete as for (B).

Bushes and house (L)
Make and sew in place as for bushes
and houses (H).

Hill (M) and sheep

Cut hill from emerald green velvet. From light green velvet cut two strips for fields, one 1⅛in (3cm) wide and one 1¼in (3.5cm) wide. Baste and sew velvet strips and pieces of bouclé yarn to hills as for hill (G). Baste and slip stitch path (M) in place. Place pieces for sheep together in pairs. Baste and overcast together around the edges, filling slightly as you work. Brush the front side of each sheep. Work a French knot in black thread to make an eye for each sheep. Using black thread, overcast edge below eye for nose. Baste and catch-stitch sheep in place on hill. Complete hill as for hill (B).

Bushes (N and O)
Make and stitch in place as for the bushes (C).

Fence (P)

Cut four 1⅛in (3cm) squares and one 2¾ × ¾in (7 × 2cm) rectangle from brown felt. Roll up felt squares and slip stitch long edges at back for fence posts. Fold rectangle and slip stitch long edges at back for fence rail. Position fence; baste and catch-stitch in place.

Hill (Q) and cattle
1 Cut out hill from light green velvet.

2 For bull's tail, cut a strip of black felt 3⅛ × ⅜in (8 × 1cm) and a ⅜in (1cm) square of white felt. Cut a pipe cleaner in half. Roll black felt strip around pipe cleaner and slip stitch long edge at back. Roll up white felt square for tail end and cut one edge into a fringe. Encase the white fringe in tail strip. Bend tail and sew in position on hill.

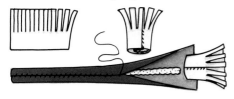

3 Baste and overcast white felt body patches in place on bull's body. Baste and overcast beige hooves to feet. Place body

over tail on hill, baste and catch-stitch in place, stuffing body as you work.

4 Baste and overcast horns together, stuffing as you work.

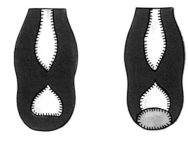

5 Baste and overcast white patches to

head front. Baste and overcast upper lip in place, filling lightly as you work.

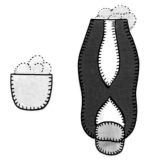

6 Place lower lips together; baste and overcast edges together, leaving top edge open. Stuff lightly. Place head front and head back together, inserting lower lip. Baste and overcast edges together, leaving top edge of head open. Stuff head

POSITION AND ORDER CHART

Terry Evans

John Hutchinson

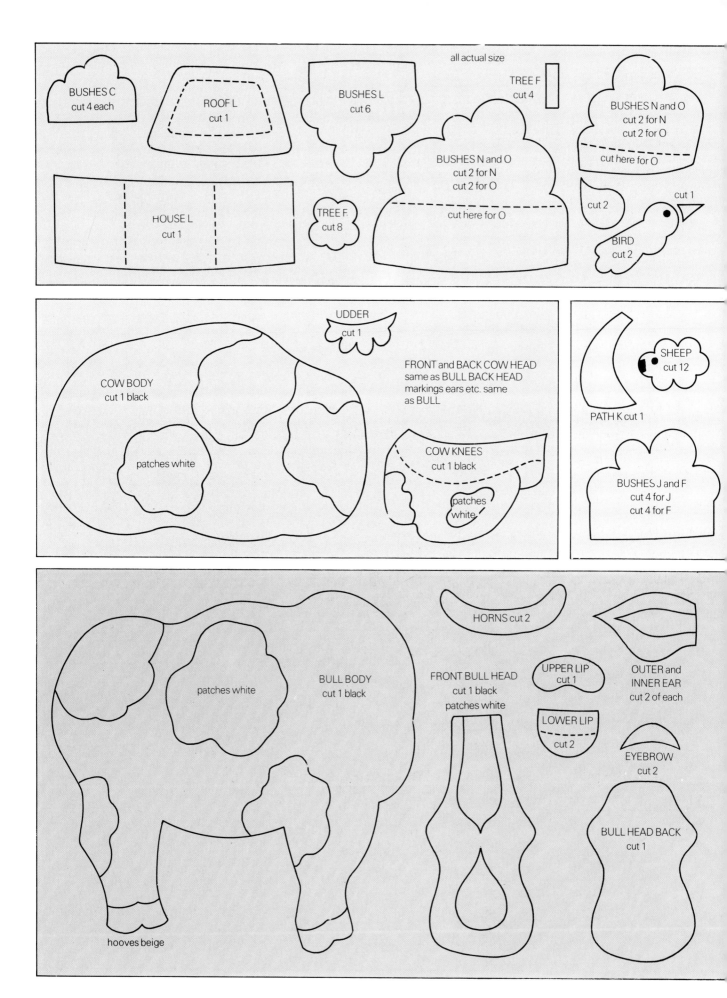

all actual size

BUSHES C
cut 4 each

ROOF L
cut 1

BUSHES L
cut 6

TREE F
cut 4

BUSHES N and O
cut 2 for N
cut 2 for O

cut here for O

HOUSE L
cut 1

TREE F.
cut 8

BUSHES N and O
cut 2 for N
cut 2 for O

cut here for O

cut 2

cut 1

BIRD
cut 2

UDDER
cut 1

COW BODY
cut 1 black

patches white

FRONT and BACK COW HEAD
same as BULL BACK HEAD
markings ears etc. same
as BULL

COW KNEES
cut 1 black

patches
white

SHEEP
cut 12

PATH K cut 1

BUSHES J and F
cut 4 for J
cut 4 for F

HORNS cut 2

patches white

BULL BODY
cut 1 black

FRONT BULL HEAD
cut 1 black
patches white

UPPER LIP
cut 1

OUTER and
INNER EAR
cut 2 of each

LOWER LIP
cut 2

EYEBROW
cut 2

BULL HEAD BACK
cut 1

hooves beige

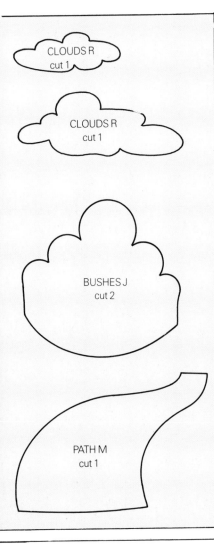

CLOUDS R
cut 1

CLOUDS R
cut 1

BUSHES J
cut 2

PATH M
cut 1

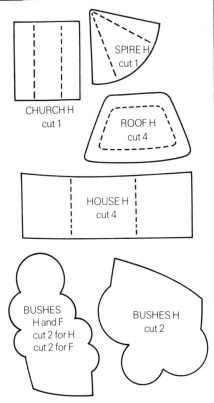

CHURCH H
cut 1

SPIRE H
cut 1

ROOF H
cut 4

HOUSE H
cut 4

BUSHES
H and F
cut 2 for H
cut 2 for F

BUSHES H
cut 2

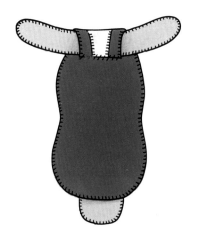

2 Position bird on hill (Q), baste and catch-stitch in place. Stitch flowers in place on hill (Q). Set hill (Q) in place and complete as for hill (B). Couch stitch two lines of bouclé yarn along edge of hilltop.

3 Position clouds in sky and overcast in place.

7 Fold top front head to back, over horns; stitch in place at back.

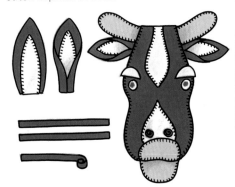

8 Cut two narrow strips of black felt about $\frac{1}{4} \times \frac{1}{8}$in (5×3mm) for nostrils. Roll up each strip; stitch in place. Catch-stitch eyebrows to head, around eye sockets. Push glass eyes into eye sockets, stitching wires flat at back of head.
9 Place inner ears on outer ears. Fold combined ears over at bases; stitch at each side of head, positioning each at a different angle.
10 Baste and catch-stitch head to body Brush face and body to make the animal fluffy.
11 Make cow the same way as the bull, stitching the knees in place at the same time as the tail. Position udder and hoof and overcast in place.

Birds, flowers and clouds

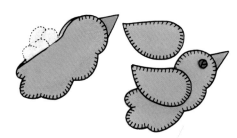

1 Place bird body pieces together. Baste and overcast edges together, stuffing bird as you work and catching in beak at front. Make the wing the same way. Sew wing to body. Using black thread work a French knot on head for eye.

Finishing

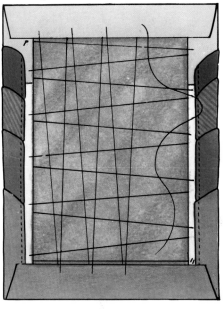

Center the completed collage on the board, pull edges over to wrong side; lace edges together with strong thread. Turn in $\frac{3}{4}$in (2cm) all around remaining piece of backing fabric. Place it on back of board; slip stitch, covering the raw edges. Attach screw rings and hanging cord.

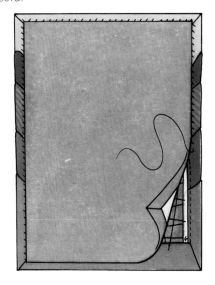

John Hutchinson

Terry Evans

Homemaker

Crisp and charming

Ruffled sheer curtains give an appealing, fresh look to a window. You can make them short or long, let them hang straight, tie them back or—for a lavish look—drape one curtain elegantly over the other.

Ruffles can be used on various kinds of curtain but are most usual on sheer curtains which tie back, sometimes crossing over in the center. The depth of the ruffle should be in proportion to the curtain and window size; for example, a very deep ruffle would not normally be used on a small window. As a general rule, ruffles are 3-6in (7.5-15cm) deep.

Making ruffled curtains

1 Before you can estimate the fabric required you must calculate the cutting size of the ruffle. Decide on the finished ruffle depth required and add $1\frac{1}{4}$in (3cm) for hems.
To determine the length of the ruffle allow between two and a half and three times the finished ruffle length (usually the sum of one side and bottom edge of the curtain, as these are the edges ruffled on most curtains). If several pieces have to be joined to make the ruffle, add small seam allowances for each joining.
2 Measure the width and depth of the window and calculate the size of the curtain as you would for one without ruffles. Add $1\frac{1}{2}$-2in (4-5cm) to the width for the side hems and add small seam allowances if panels of fabric have to be joined. From this total, subtract the finished ruffle depth to find the cutting width of the curtain itself. To determine the cutting length of the curtain: take the finished length, then add $\frac{5}{8}$in (1.5cm) for a seam and a suitable allowance for the type of heading you are using (see "Sheer elegance," Volume 3, pages 120-123). From this total, subtract the depth of the finished ruffle.
3 Cut out the curtains and the ruffle pieces to the measurements you have obtained. Always cut the ruffle as long as possible to avoid too many seams, as these will stand out because of the sheerness of the fabric.
4 Join the panels for the curtains if necessary. If ruffle pieces have to be joined, use narrow interlocking fell seams (see Volume 3, page 122).
The ruffle can be attached to the curtain in either of two ways, depending on the heading used.

Plain casing curtains

1 Turn under and stitch a narrow double hem on one long edge of the ruffle.

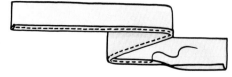

2 On the other long edge, stitch two rows of gathering stitches close to the raw edge.

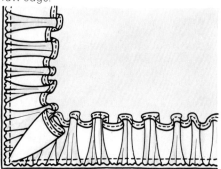

3 Pull up the gathering threads until the ruffle fits the edges of the curtain. Pin and baste the ruffle to the curtain with right sides together and gathers evenly distributed. Stitch the two pieces together between the two lines of gathering stitches.

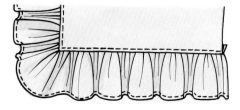

4 Press the seams toward the curtain. On the right side topstitch close to the seam through all thicknesses. Finish the seam if necessary.

Headed casing curtains

1 Turn under and stitch narrow double hems on both long edges of the ruffle.
2 Baste and stitch narrow double hems to the right side on the inner and bottom edges of the curtain.

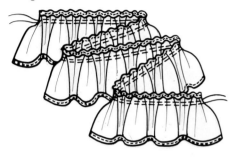

3 Stitch two lines of gathering stitches, 1in (2.5cm) from one long edge of ruffle.

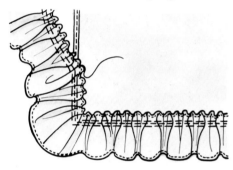

4 Pull up the gathering threads to fit the two edges of the curtain. Pin the ruffle to the curtain with right sides facing upward and the gathering stitches over the hem on the curtain. Make sure the ruffle is evenly distributed around both edges and does not look skimped at the corner. Stitch the ruffle in place, stitching over the gathering threads on the right side.

Finishing both types of curtain

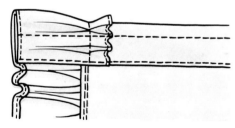

1 Turn under and stitch double hems at the outer curtain edge.
2 Turn under and stitch the casings at the top of the curtain as explained in Volume 3, page 123, extending the casing across the ruffle.

114

Cross-over tie-back curtains

Tie-back curtains which cross over each other for part or all of the window width give a lavish look to the window at relatively little cost. The success of the curtains will depend on how well the fabric drapes. Sheer fabrics are ideal for cross-overs because the folds of the curtain underneath can be seen through those of the curtain on top. Generally, this type of curtain is finished with a ruffle. The instructions that follow are for ruffled cross-overs. However, you may adapt them for plain cross-overs by not subtracting the ruffle allowances and by adding, instead, allowances for two side hems and a lower hem.

Making cross-over curtains

1 To estimate the total fabric width needed for the window, first decide where you want the curtains to cross. Then measure the finished, gathered length of curtain. For example, if the curtain rod is 80in (202cm) long and each curtain will go across two-thirds of the rod, the finished, gathered width of each curtain is about 53in (135cm). Subtract the depth of the ruffle. Double the resulting figure (for the two curtains), then multiply it by 2 or 3 for the desired fullness. Add 4in (10cm) for outer side hem allowances and 1in (2.5cm) for each seam if fabric panels have to be joined.
2 Estimate the length of the curtains by measuring from the rod to $\frac{1}{2}$in (1.2cm) above the floor, if you are making floor length curtains, or to the sill or just below it for short curtains. Add a top heading allowance, and subtract the depth of the ruffle.

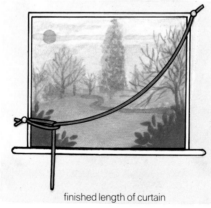

finished length of curtain

3 If your windows are very wide and you want the curtains to cross over the entire width, you may have to cut the inside edge longer than the outside edge in order to have enough fabric to drape. Pin one end of a piece of string to the window frame where the inner edge of the curtain will start. Drape the string over to the side of the window where the curtains will be held by the tie-back, allowing the fullness desired. Decide on

the finished curtain length below the tie-back and mark this point on the string. Measure the string to find the finished curtain length. Add a heading allowance to this figure, and subtract the depth of the ruffle. Estimate the length of the outer edge without draping, in the usual way.

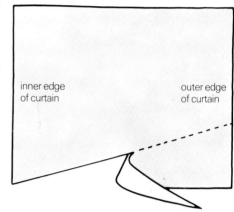

inner edge of curtain

outer edge of curtain

4 Cut out all the widths of fabric to the longer length and join the panels for each curtain. On one curtain mark the shorter measurement on the outside edge. Chalk a diagonal line to join this point to the inner corner of the curtain. Trim away the fabric below the line. Cut out the other curtain using the first as a pattern, placing the right sides together and making sure that any pattern in the fabric is level on both.
Note This method is suitable only for curtains with ruffles, as a deep hem will not hang properly if turned up on a diagonal.
5 Add ruffles as instructed above. Hem the outer sides of each curtain. (Or hem both sides and the lower edge, if you are making plain curtains.)
6 Turn under and stitch the headings separately on each curtain if you wish to use two separate rods.

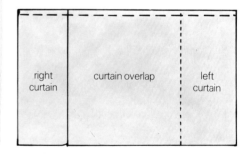

right curtain

curtain overlap

left curtain

7 If you are hanging both panels on a single rod, lay the two curtains together with right sides upward, overlapping them by the amount required. Double check that they still fit the width of the window.
Turn under and stitch a casing along the whole width of the curtains, treating the double fabric where the curtains overlap as a single layer so that the two curtains will slip onto one rod.

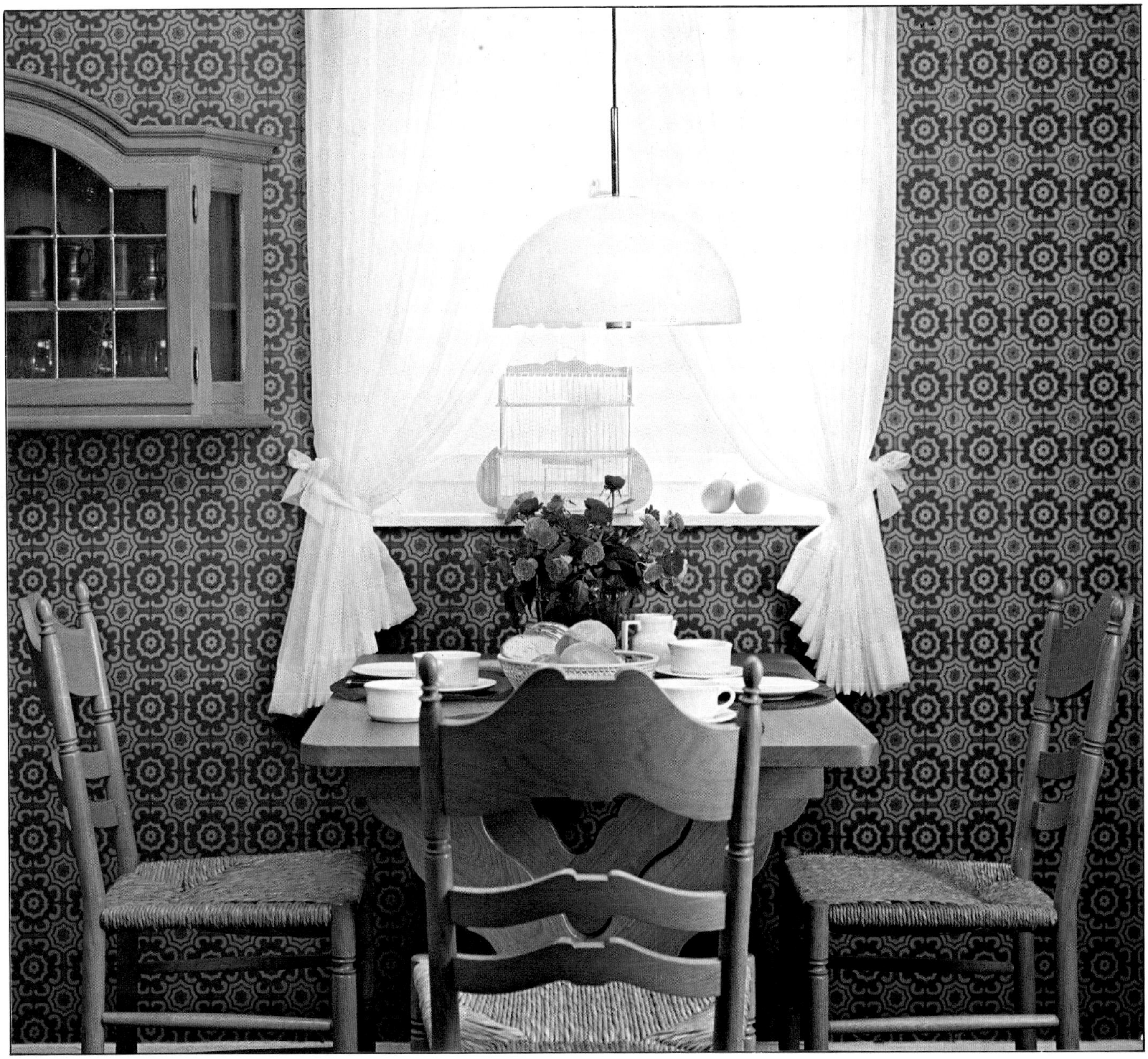

Camera Press

Tie-backs

Tie-backs are the finishing touch to ruffled curtains and should be made with the size and style of the curtains in mind. We give instructions for simple tie-backs, but you can, if you prefer, make shaped or ruffled tie-backs.

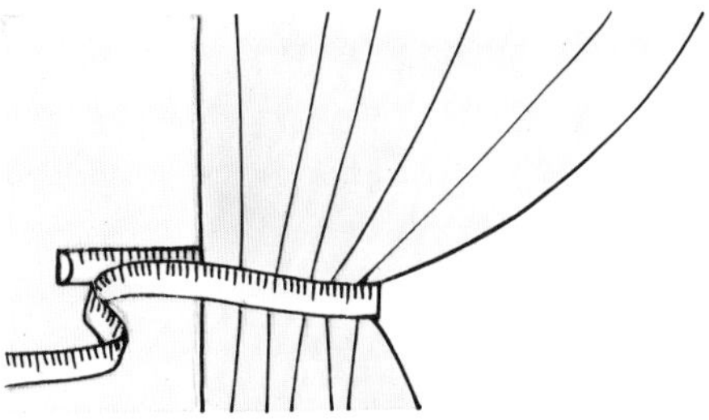

1 To determine how long your tie-backs should be, hang the curtains up and loop a tapemeasure around the curtain, draping it to the side of the window. Allow sufficient room in the tie-back for the curtains to hang well. Add $\frac{3}{4}$in (2cm) for seams to the finished length of the tie-back.

2 Decide on the width of the tie-back. Make a paper pattern of the finished dimensions and try it against the curtains. Make any necessary adjustment. Add $\frac{3}{4}$in (2cm) seam allowances to the finished width measurement.

3 Cut out two strips of fabric to the measurements you have worked out for each tie-back.

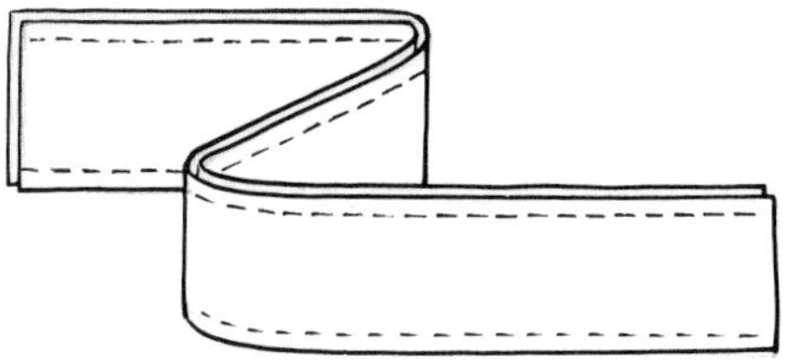

4 Stitch the two pieces together along the long edges taking $\frac{3}{8}$in (1cm) seams and making sure that the right sides are facing. Trim seam allowances and turn strip right side out.

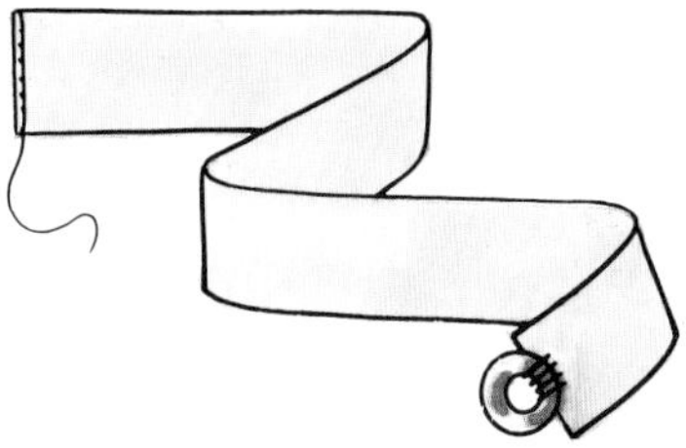

Terry Evans

5 Turn in the seam allowances on the short ends and slipstitch the folded edges together. Attach a small ring near each end of the tie-back. Fix a small hook to the window frame to hold the tie-back in place.

Make the other tie-back in the same way.

Homemaker

Toy town

Finished size
Each building is about 10¼in (26cm) tall.

Materials (for all buildings)
  ⅜yd (.3m) of 36in (90cm)-wide
    white cotton lining fabric
  Piece of white felt 23¼ x 8in
    (60 x 20cm)
  Piece of brown felt 10 x 6in (25 x
    15cm)
  Three pieces of felt, each 31½ x 12in
    (80 x 30cm) in red, blue and yellow
  Tapestry yarn in brown, red, yellow
    and green
  Stranded embroidery floss in blue,
    green and red
  Suitable stuffing
  Tracing paper; pencil
  Dressmaker's carbon paper

"Thatched" cottage

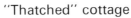

1 Using tracing paper and a sharp pencil, trace all the patterns for the cottage from page 118.
2 Using dressmaker's carbon paper, mark the complete cottage front on one side of cotton lining fabric. Cut out complete front.

3 Using dressmaker's carbon mark the doors, roofs, etc., on the appropriate colored felts. Also mark a front wall in white felt. Cut out the pieces.

Three little pillows decorated with felt and embroidery make a mini-village for a toddler.

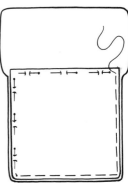

4 Lay the white felt front wall over the bottom half of the cotton fabric. Pin and baste to fabric.

5 Lay the brown felt roof piece over the cotton lining fabric with the lower edge overlapping the top of the white felt wall. Pin and baste to the lining fabric.

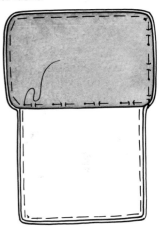

6 Using matching sewing thread, stitch across the lower edge of the roof, catching in white felt front wall and lining fabric.
7 Carefully measure, pin, baste and stitch along seamline, from edge, to give a boundary for the embroidery.

117

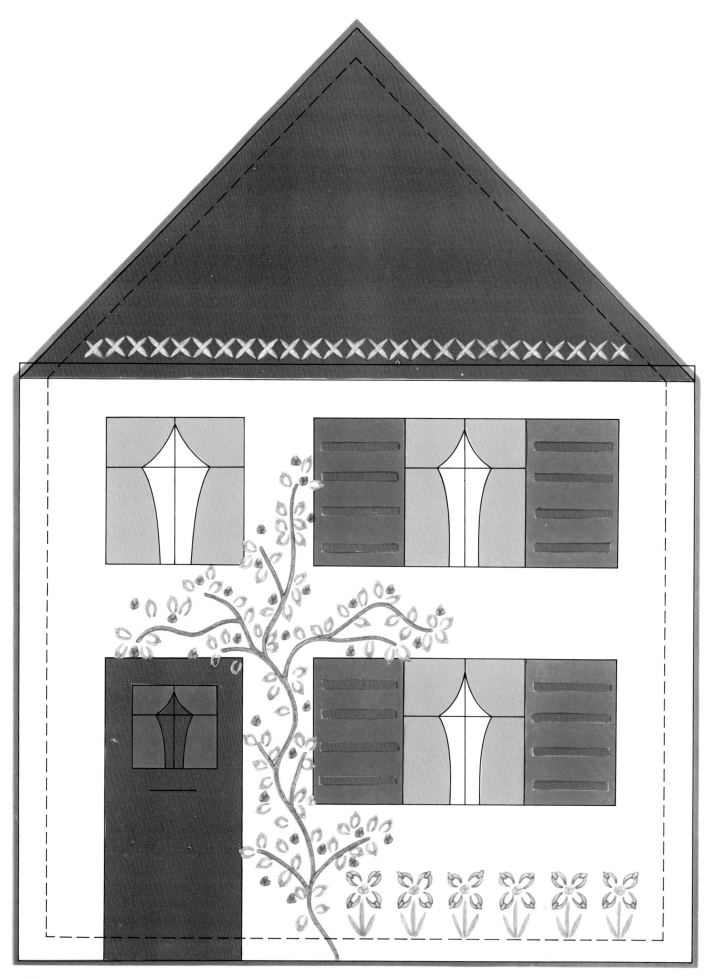

8 Using the original pattern on page 118 as a guide, place door and windows in position on white felt front wall. Pin, baste and stitch around door and windows close to the edges, using matching sewing thread.

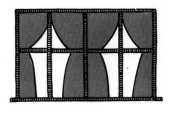

9 Using black thread and with the sewing machine set to satin stitch, stitch around the edges of the window and door window. Repeat across all windows at right angles to complete the window frames.

10 Stitch a short bar in the same way under the window on the door, for a mail slot.

11 Using pencil and following the original pattern on page 118, mark the climbing vine on the white felt front wall between the door and window. Stitch the stem in the same way as the letter box, but use brown sewing thread.

12 Pull all the loose ends from the machine embroidery to the wrong side and either tie them securely or darn them into the work.

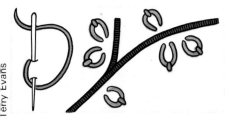

13 Using green stranded embroidery floss, work the leaves on each side of the vine in detached chain stitch.

14 Work the cherries in French knots using red tapestry yarn.

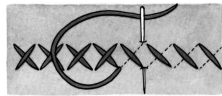

15 Work a row of cross stitch in brown tapestry yarn across the top of the roof.

16 Work a row of flowers along the base boundary line from the climbing vine to the outer edge, using green, blue and red stranded embroidery floss. Work blue flowers in daisy stitch and use straight stitches in green for the stems and leaves, with red French knots for the centers.

17 From yellow felt cut out a strip 31½ x 4in (80 x 10cm) for the side gusset.

18 Pin gusset around front of cottage with right sides together following boundary stitching line, so that the short edges of the gusset meet at the center of the base. Pin, baste and stitch the short edges of gusset together to fit. Cut away any excess seam allowance leaving ⅜in (1cm) on each end of gusset. Baste and stitch all around on stitching line.

19 Pin, baste and stitch back of house to opposite long edge of gusset in the same way, leaving a 4in (10cm) opening in the base.

20 Turn the cottage right side out. Stuff cottage firmly. Turn in the edges of the opening and slip stitch neatly to close the opening.

Fruit store

1 Make the store the same way as for the cottage, following steps 1 to 7.

2 Using the original pattern on page 119 as a guide, place door, window and large front window in position on white felt front wall. Pin, baste and stitch around door, window and large front window, close to edges, in matching sewing thread.

3 Stitch around windows and door and make mail slot in satin stitch as for cottage, steps 9 and 10.

4 Using yellow tapestry yarn, work a row of cross stitch across the top of the roof.

5 Using red tapestry yarn, work a line of cross-stitch across the top of the awning.

6 Work the fruit in the large front window in French knots using yellow, green and red tapestry yarn.

7 Work a row of cross-stitch flowers along the base boundary line below the large front window in red tapestry yarn with the stems and leaves in straight stitch using green tapestry yarn.

8 Finish the fruit store as for the cottage, steps 17 to 20, but cutting side gusset strip from blue felt.

House

1 Make the house in the same way as for the cottage, following steps 1 to 7.

2 Using the original pattern on the opposite page as a guide, place door, three windows and two pairs of shutters in position on white felt front wall. Pin, baste and stitch around door, windows and shutters close to edges in matching sewing thread.

3 Stitch around windows and make mail slot in satin stitch as for cottage, steps 9 and 10.

4 Stitch four satin stitch bars in red sewing thread across each of the blue shutters.

5 Using blue embroidery floss work a line of cross-stitch across lower edge of roof.

6 Mark the climbing vine and work leaves and cherries in the same way as for the cottage, steps 11 to 14.

7 Work a row of flowers along the base boundary line from the vine to the outer edge. Work the flowers in daisy stitch using yellow tapestry yarn, and stems and leaves using green embroidery floss in straight stitches. Use blue embroidery floss for French knots in the centers.

8 Finish the house as for the cottage, steps 17 to 20, but cutting side gusset strip from red felt.

Terry Evans

Homemaker

Bright and breezy

Protect yourself from brisk on-shore winds with our colorful windbreak . . . or use it to provide a handy changing area.

Size
49in (126cm) high, about 11⅓ft (3.45m) long.

Materials
2yd (1.8m) of 36in (90cm)-wide blue heavyweight cotton fabric
2⅞yd (2.6m) of 36in (90cm)-wide yellow heavyweight cotton fabric
2⅞yd (2.6m) of 36in (90cm)-wide red heavyweight cotton fabric
2 heavy-duty snaps, thread, knife
5 lengths of ⅝in (1.5cm)-diameter dowel 4ft 3in (1.6m) long

Cutting out
1 For main panel pieces, cut one piece 51 × 36in (130×90cm) from both blue and red fabrics. Cut two pieces, each 51 × 36in (130×90cm), from yellow.
2 For dowel casings, cut ten strips, each 26 × 2¾in (66×7cm), from red fabric.
3 Cut out two pockets 13¼ × 12in (34×30.5cm) from red and blue fabrics.

Casing and pockets

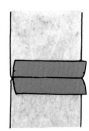

1 To make complete casing length, the casing pieces will have to be joined together. Place casing strips together in pairs, with right sides facing. Pin, baste and sew one short edge of each pair, making ½in (1cm) seam. Open out and press seams open. From the wrong side sew across each casing strip again, along each seam allowance, close to seam. This makes the five casing strips each 51in (130cm) long.

Gary Warren

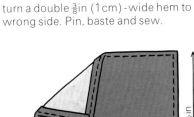

2 At short ends of each casing strip, turn a double ⅜in (1cm) - wide hem to wrong side. Pin, baste and sew.

Pin, baste and topstitch all around, ¼in (5mm) from folded edge, using blue thread on red pocket and yellow thread on blue pocket.

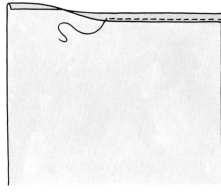

3 For each pocket, turn ¾in (2cm) to the wrong side, all around each pocket piece.

4 On raw edges of each panel piece, turn a ⅜in (1cm) - wide double hem to wrong side. Pin, baste and sew down.

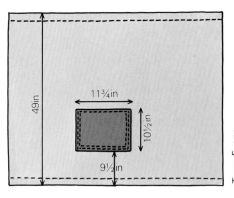

11¾in

49in

10½in

9½in

Terry Evans

5 Place red pocket right side up on right side of yellow panel, equidistant from side edges and 9½in (24cm) from lower edge. Pin, baste and topstitch in place, ⅜in (1cm) from side and bottom edges of pocket, using blue thread.

6 Position and stitch blue pocket on right side of red panel in the same way, using yellow thread.

Handle

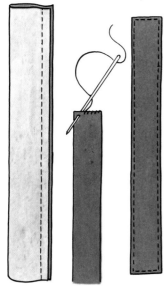

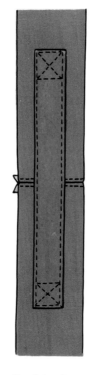

1 For handle, from blue fabric cut one strip 11 × 3in (28 × 8cm). Fold in half lengthwise, right sides facing; pin, baste and sew long edges, ⅜in (1cm) from raw edge. Turn handle right side out and press seam over center. Turn in ⅜in (1cm) at each short edge; pin, baste and slip stitch folded edges together. Topstitch around handle about ¼in (5mm) from outer edge, using yellow thread.

2 Center handle, right side up, over the seamline on right side of one casing piece, ¾in (2cm) from each long raw edge. Pin, baste and topstitch each handle end in place as shown, going over previous topstitching lines where appropriate.

Assembling

1 Fold each casing strip in half lengthwise, with wrong sides facing. Pin and baste down complete length, ⅜in (1cm) from raw edges.

2 Place one casing piece (without handle) on right side of blue panel, with raw edges of casing parallel to one selvage of panel ⅜in (1cm) from edge. Pin, baste and sew in place.

Gary Warren

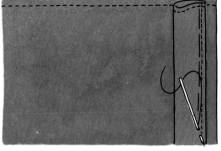

3 Place another casing (without handle) along opposite selvage edge of blue panel in the same way. Pin and baste in place but do not sew.

4 With right sides facing, match selvage of yellow panel with red pocket to the selvage of blue panel on which casing was just basted, making sure casing lies flat along panel. Pin, baste and sew in place ¾in (2cm) from edge, catching in raw edges of the casing.

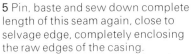

5 Pin, baste and sew down complete length of this seam again, close to selvage edge, completely enclosing the raw edges of the casing.

6 To stitch first the red and then the second plain yellow panel in place, repeat steps 2-5, each time catching one plain casing piece between panel pieces and each time finishing the seam.

7 To attach casing with handle to the remaining selvage of last yellow panel, match pieces as in step 2. Pin, baste and sew casing in place.

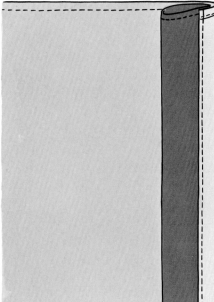

8 To finish seams at each outer edge, turn selvage edge of panel piece over raw edges of casing. Pin, baste and sew down complete length.

Finishing

1 For fastening strap, from remaining blue fabric cut a strip 27 × 3in (68.5 × 7.5cm). Fold in half lengthwise with right sides facing. Pin, baste and sew long edges together, ⅜in (1cm) from raw edges. Turn strap right side out and press. Turn in ⅜in (1cm) at each short edge; slip stitch folded edges together. Topstitch around strap about ¼in (5mm) from outer edges, using yellow thread.

2 To attach strap, place at right angles to end casing (with handle), matching center of strap to seam of casing. Pin, baste and sew strap securely to casing as shown.

3 Attach snaps to strap, ¾in (2cm) and 4in (10cm) from short ends.

4 Using sharp knife, sharpen one end of each length of dowel. Insert a length of dowel down each casing, with sharpened ends pointed downward.

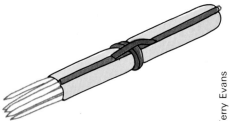

Terry Evans

5 When windbreak is not in use, roll it up from end opposite handle; wrap strap around roll twice and fasten in place.

Homemaker

Keep a note

This memo board is very handy for keeping notes and bills together.

Materials

Four 12in (30cm) square cork tiles
Pieces of felt, each 20 x 14in
   (50 x 35cm), in red. blue, light
   green and yellow
Piece of apple green felt 14 x 6in
   (35 x 15cm)
Piece of brown felt 20 x 2¼in
   (50 x 6cm)
Scraps of dark green felt
1¾yd (1.5m) of red ball fringe (or
   length from which 31 balls can be
   cut)
Sheet of backing cardboard 24 x 20in
   (60 x 51cm)
Sheet of paper 24 x 20in (60 x 51cm)
Glue; sharp craft knife
Thin cardboard; tracing paper
Dressmaker's carbon paper
Matching sewing thread
Two screw eyes
Nylon picture-hanging cord

1 Trace the patterns for treetops, trunks, leaves, sun and grass from page 128. Using dressmaker's carbon, mark the patterns on one side of the appropriate colored felts, the number of times stated.

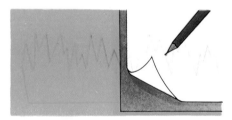

2 To gain the full width of the grass, mark the pattern twice across the light green felt: fold a strip of light green felt in half; pin together around edges; mark the pattern on one side, positioning the broken line on the fold. Cut out through both layers.

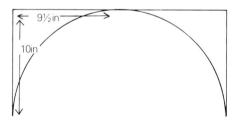

3 Cut a curve around the top of the backing cardboard. Mark two points 9½in (24cm) in from each corner on one edge. Similarly, mark off 10in (25cm) down each side. Draw a curved line, joining up the two points on each side.

4 To make the patterns for the rainbow arcs, place the cardboard shape on the piece of paper and mark around; remove the cardboard. On the paper shape, draw three more arcs ⅝in (1.5cm) apart inside the curved top edge. Place the felt treetops and trunks in position at each side of paper shape with base and sides matching. Draw around treetop, where it meets the rainbow arcs. Remove trees. Carefully cut out the rainbow arc patterns.
5 Cut out the rainbow arcs in felt; working from the outside, use blue, red, light green and yellow felts.

6 Cut 31 balls off the red ball fringe. To make apples, hand sew leaves to each ball, mixing light and dark greens on some of the balls.

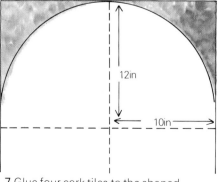

7 Glue four cork tiles to the shaped backing cardboard, matching the base

Jay Myrdal

edges and centering the vertical join. Place a firm weight on the cork tiles and leave to dry.

8 When glue is dry, use a sharp-pointed craft knife to cut excess cork from around the curved and side edges. Work from cardboard side for a smooth edge.

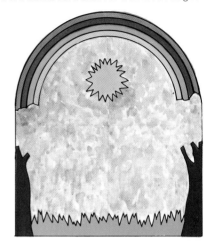

9 Now working with the cork side facing you, glue tree trunks in place, matching the base and side edges of the board.
10 Place the grass strip along the base edge. Trim away excess at tree trunks. Glue in place.
11 Glue the rainbow arcs in place around the curved top edge of the board, starting with the outer strip and working inward. Make sure each arc butts against the next one.
12 Glue the sun to the cork just below the rainbow.

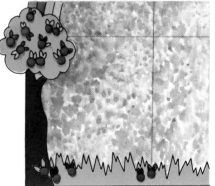

Terri Lawlor

13 Glue the felt treetops to the thin cardboard. When glue is dry, working from the felt side, cut away excess cardboard from around the felt. Glue the treetops in place at the top of the tree trunks. They will extend beyond the side edges of the board.
14 Arrange and glue the apples onto the treetops, adding any extra leaves, and also onto the grass, along the lower edge of the board.
15 For hanging, fix the screw eyes into the back of the board. Thread a length of nylon picture cord through the eyes and knot ends together securely.

SUN
cut 1 in yellow

GRASS
cut 2 in light green

TREETOPS
cut 2 in apple green

LEFT TREE TRUNK
cut 1 in brown

RIGHT TREE TRUNK
cut 1 in brown

fold

John Hutchinson